Industrial Clusters and Micro and Small Enterprises in Africa

Industrial Clusters and Micro and Small Enterprises in Africa

From Survival to Growth

Yutaka Yoshino, Editor

A report based on joint research by the World Bank, the Japan International Cooperation Agency, the Foundation for Advanced Studies on International Development, and economists affiliated with the African Economic Research Consortium.

THE WORLD BANK
Washington, D.C.

ISBN: 978-0-8213-8627-9
eISBN: 978-0-8213-8628-6
DOI: 10.1596/978-0-8213-8627-9

Library of Congress Cataloging-in-Publication Data
Industrial clusters and micro and small enterprises in Africa : from survival to growth/ Yutaka Yoshino, editor.
  p. cm.
  Includes bibliographical references and index.
  ISBN 978-0-8213-8627-9 — ISBN 978-0-8213-8628-6 (electronic)
  1. Industrial clusters—Africa. 2. Small business—Africa. 3. Business enterprises—Africa. 4. Industrialization—Africa. I. World Bank.
  HC800.Z9D555 2010
  338.8'7—dc22

                                                                    2010047884

Cover photo by Yutaka Yoshino.
Cover design by Quantum Think.

Contents

Boxes

Figures

Tables

Foreword

The history of economic development around the world teaches us that industrialization is a key driver of growth. Yet the vast majority of African economies have yet to see their manufacturing sector develop and thereby contribute to sustained growth. In Sub-Saharan African countries, manufacturing on average takes up only 14 percent of GDP, in sharp contrast to 32 percent among low- and middle-income East Asian economies. Natural resources and agricultural commodities dominate African exports. The formal private sector is still very small. In short, African industrialization is arguably the biggest challenge facing Africa's development.

This is not to say that manufacturing is absent in Africa. In fact, there is a dynamic, indigenous manufacturing sector, perhaps not fully reflected in official statistics. When I first visited Africa as the new chief economist of the World Bank, I was struck by the untapped potential of small entrepreneurs, often operating in an informal setting. In every major commercial city, concentrations of micro and small enterprises are engaged in a range of manufacturing activities—from metalwork to carpentry and furniture making, from garments to food making. Those enterprises constitute the lion's share of manufacturers in the region. They are also potential sources of employment, skill development, and therefore poverty reduction.

This study—prepared in a partnership of the World Bank, the Japan International Cooperation Agency, the Foundation for Advanced Studies on International Development, and economists affiliated with the African Economic Research Consortium—is one of the first attempts to conduct a comprehensive quantitative assessment of the performance of enterprises in industrial clusters in Africa. The researchers collected original data from a set of industrial clusters in Africa, focusing on naturally formed clusters in light manufacturing industries. The analysis highlights key potentials and growth constraints of such clusters. Unlike more advanced, innovation-oriented clusters often observed in other regions, most clusters in Africa are still at subsistence level—what we call "survival clusters." Observing the significance of entrepreneurial skills and knowledge to overcome such growth constraints, the study takes an innovative approach by conducting a series of scientifically designed and evaluated field experiments that provide management training programs to cluster-based entrepreneurs.

Whether or not micro and small enterprises contribute to industrialization has been a topic of debate. Some say that African industrialization cannot take off without sufficient growth in foreign investment and large enterprises. Without negating the importance of foreign investors and large enterprises, this study emphasizes the critical role that small enterprises play in establishing a broad base of domestic manufacturing. As seen in several Asian countries, small enterprises could develop important linkages between local economies and foreign investors and large enterprises. African governments are increasingly keen on formulating proactive policies to develop competitive domestic industries. By empirically assessing the potentials and constraints of clusters that have been formed naturally without particular government policies, the study contributes to a better understanding of what roles policies should play in the process of clustering for industrialization and, ultimately, in the transformation of the African continent.

Justin Yifu Lin
Senior Vice President, Development Economics
and Chief Economist
World Bank

Acknowledgments

This report is the output of the African Enterprise Study, implemented jointly by the World Bank team led by Yutaka Yoshino, the Japan International Cooperation Agency (JICA) team led by Megumi Muto, and the Foundation for Advanced Studies on International Development (FASID) team led by Tetsushi Sonobe. Other members of the team include Asya Akhlaque, Vivian Agbegha, Theophile Bougna, Rosanna Chan, Michael Engman, Juan Feng, Manuella Frota, Varun Kshirsagar, Taye Mengistae, and Mallika Shakya from the World Bank; Yessica Chung, Shinobu Shimokoshi, Asami Takeda, and Ryo Ochiai from JICA; and Keijiro Otsuka and Yukichi Mano from FASID.

The study was produced in partnership with researchers affiliated with the African Economic Research Consortium (AERC), who conducted the country case studies on industrial clusters. Olusanya Ajakaiye provided overall guidance and facilitation. The Institute of Policy Analysis and Research, Kenya (IPAR-Kenya) conducted the study for Kenya, led by John Akoten, currently with the Ministry of Industrialization, Kenya; the Institute of Policy Analysis and Research, Rwanda (IPAR-Rwanda) conducted the study for Rwanda, led by Serge Musana; the Institute of Statistical Social and Economic Research (ISSER) conducted the study for Ghana, led by Peter Quartey and George Owusu; Sunday Khan

(University of Yaounde II) conducted the study for Cameroon; and Vinaye Ancharaz (University of Mauritius) conducted the study for Mauritius.

John Akoten (Ministry of Industrialization, Kenya) and Alhassan Iddrisu (Ministry of Finance and Planning, Ghana) supported the implementation of experimental training programs in Nairobi, Kenya, and Kumasi, Ghana, respectively. The team of trainers from EDC Consulting Limited (Accra, Ghana), led by Abena Otu, conducted the training programs. Elizabeth White (World Bank) and Johane Rajaobelina (International Finance Corporation) contributed to preparation of the training programs.

The study was conducted under the overall guidance of Shantayanan Devarajan and Marilou Uy of the World Bank as well as John Page (Brookings Institution). The team also benefited from the guidance of Hiroto Arakawa and Keiichi Tsunekawa of JICA. Peer reviewers were Benno Ndulu (Bank of Tanzania, concept stage), Vincent Palmade (World Bank), Hinh Dinh (World Bank), Thomas Farole (World Bank), and Vijaya Ramachandran (Center for Global Development).

The report was edited by Yutaka Yoshino (World Bank) based on the background papers and other inputs provided by members of the joint teams listed above.

Valuable comments were received from a large number of people on the report manuscript as well as on the background papers. The team would like to thank members of the World Bank Africa Labor Market Analysis Group, including Louise Fox, who chaired the session; participants of the brown-bag seminar, including discussants Vincent Palmade, Dino Merotto, and Papa Demba Thiam; Francis Teal (University of Oxford) and Arne Bigsten (Gothenburg University), who provided comments on the concept note of the project; the discussants and the participants at the Tokyo International Conference on African Development IV seminar (Yokohama, Japan, May 29, 2008), the Annual Bank Conference on Development Economics breakfast seminar (Cape Town, South Africa, June 10, 2008), the AERC Biannual Workshop (Nairobi, Kenya, December 1, 2009), including Hon. Joe Baidoe-Ansah (Ghana), Ephraim Njega Mumbi (Kenya Association of Young Entrepreneurs), Olusanya Ajakaiye (AERC), Samuel Nyantahe (Daima Associates in Tanzania), and Jorge Arbache (World Bank), for comments on the early findings of the study; and the session chair, discussant, and participants at the AERC, JICA, and World Bank Senior Policy Seminar (Nairobi, Kenya, May 7, 2010) and the African Development Bank and JICA seminar (Abidjan,

Côte d'Ivoire, May 25, 2010), including Hon. Mahama Ayariga (Ministry of Trade and Industry, Ghana), Kevit Desai (Kenya Private Sector Alliance), and Samuel Maimbo (World Bank), for comments on the final findings of the study. Helpful suggestions were also received from Douglas Zeng, Leonardo Iacovone, Mary Hallward-Driemeier, George Clarke, Giuseppe Iarossi, Manju Shah, Francois Nankobogo, Musabi Muteshi, Yira Mascaro, Kofi-Boateng Agyen, Khoudijah Bibi Maudarbocus-Boodoo, Chunlin Zhang, Vandana Chandra, Somik Lall, Biff Steel, Nancy Benjamin, and Harold Alderman during various stages of the process.

The World Bank Office of the Publisher, External Affairs, handled the production and printing of this book under the guidance of Denise Bergeron, Susan Graham, and Stephen McGroarty. Valerie Ziobro edited an earlier draft as well as the background papers.

The team appreciates support given by Ann Karasanyi, Ken Omondi, Parveen Moses, Nana Konadu Afram-M'Bow, Amma Esson, Esther Kangethe, Nicholas Mate Runyenje, Francis Kiumbi Muthike, and Mika Iwasaki in implementing various activities under this study.

The team appreciates financial support for implementing the study that was provided by the Government of Japan through its Policy and Human Resources Development Trust Fund and the Japan Consultant Trust Fund. Funding for completing the report was also received from the Multilateral Donor Trust Fund for Trade and Development.

Abbreviations

AERC	African Economic Research Consortium
ATT	average treatment of treated
BCM	bias-corrected matching
BDS	business development services
CES	constant elasticity of substitution
DEA	data envelopment analysis
DID	differences-in-differences
EPZ	export-processing zone
FASID	Foundation for Advanced Studies on International Development
FDI	foreign direct investment
GDP	gross domestic product
ICT	information and communications technology
IDA	International Development Association
IFC	International Finance Corporation
IPAR	Institute of Policy Analysis and Research
ISO	International Organization for Standardization
ISSER	Institute of Statistical Social and Economic Research
IT	information technology
IV	instrumental variable

JICA	Japan International Cooperation Agency
MAPSKID	Master Plan Study for Kenya's Industrial Development
MSE	micro and small enterprises
OLS	ordinary least squares
PPP	purchasing power parity
PSM	propensity score matching
RedLAC	Latin American Cluster Network
RPED	Regional Program on Enterprise Development
SME	small and medium enterprises
WBES	World Bank Enterprise Survey

Overview

The private sector is the engine of economic growth, stimulating entre-preneurship and innovation and promoting competition and productiv-ity. While many countries in Africa have developed private sector–driven growth strategies, private investment as a proportion of GDP is only 13 percent in Africa, significantly lower than in other regions, such as South Asia, with many low-income countries. The public sector still occupies the lion's share of economic activity in Africa.

The sparseness of the private sector base in Africa is reflected in its dual structure. The formal private sector is dominated by a small num-ber of large enterprises, often foreign owned, that generate a large share of total private sector output (see figure 1). In addition, a very large number of micro, small, and medium enterprises are owned predomi-nantly by local indigenous entrepreneurs. The development of these smaller enterprises could have a great effect on economic growth and poverty reduction.

This study addresses how industrial clusters could be a springboard for the development of Africa's micro and small enterprise sector, which constitutes the bulk of the region's indigenous private sector. The suc-cessful development of industrial clusters in Asia illustrates how small enterprises can help to drive growth led by market expansion at home

Figure 1   Aggregate Sales and Number of Enterprises in Sub-Saharan Africa, by Size of Firm

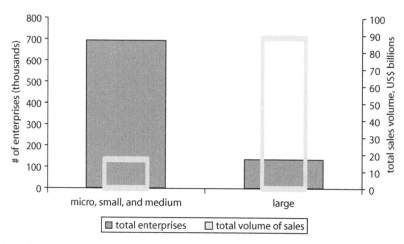

Source: Authors' estimation based on WBES data from 17 Sub-Saharan African countries, for which sample weights are available.

and abroad. The case of local garment enterprises in Zhejiang, China, shows how direct transactions with outside merchants and large customers became the drivers of growth as their product quality improved. Another example is found in Thailand, where many domestic enterprises have forged alliances with foreign enterprises to become suppliers to the export-oriented auto industry cluster in the Thai Eastern Seaboard.

Performance Gaps between Domestically Owned and Foreign-Owned Firms in Africa

Domestically owned enterprises are on average less productive than foreign-owned enterprises. This is true worldwide. In general, in Africa and elsewhere, multinational firms perform better than other enterprises, given their superior access to capital and technology. The gap, however, seems to be wider in Africa than in regions like Asia. A similar gap is observed between enterprises owned by ethnic Africans and those owned by non-African entrepreneurs.

The performance gap between domestically owned and foreign-owned firms in Africa is explained largely by the difference in firm size. Foreign-owned firms tend to have more employees and to be more productive than domestically owned firms (see figure 2). Firm size also appears to be a significant determinant of access to external markets (see figure 3). Size

Figure 2   Size and Productivity of Domestically Owned and Foreign-Owned Enterprises in Africa

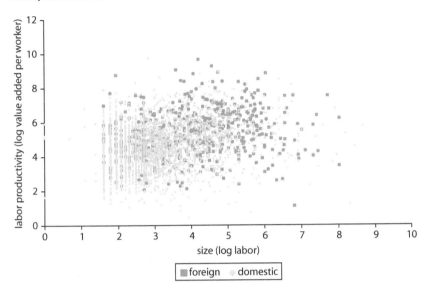

Source: Author's estimation based on WBES data.

Figure 3   Rate of Participation in Local, National, and International Sales Markets in Africa, by Nationality and Size

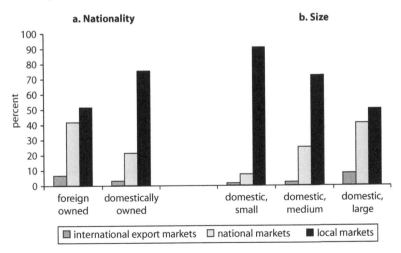

Source: Author's estimation based on WBES data.

matters both in productivity and market access, even when taking into account variations among countries and industries.

In addition to firm size, other factors also contribute to the performance gap in labor productivity (see figure 4). Capital intensity—the measure of a firm's use of physical capital relative to labor in its production—is positively correlated with labor productivity and a leading source of the performance gap. Access beyond local markets, such as national and export markets, also enhances sales performance. Studies also point to the weak educational background of managers and inadequate access to finance among micro and small enterprises in Africa as key constraints on their growth.

Although this study finds that capital intensity, market access, and managers' education are significant contributors to the foreign-domestic performance gap among firms in Africa, their contributions to the gap are less pronounced when size is taken into account. This means that a part of the effect of size on business performance is channeled through those factors.

The study further finds that the foreign-domestic gap exists simply because foreign-owned firms are more endowed with those factors than domestically owned firms. In those factors, no bias effects are observed, favoring foreign-owned firms disproportionately more than domestically owned firms. In other words, domestically owned firms would have the

Figure 4   Factors Contributing to the Foreign-Domestic Performance Gap in Africa

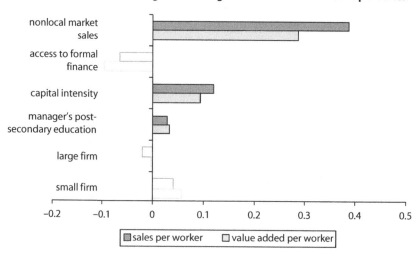

Source: Feng, Mengistae, and Yoshino 2009.
Note: Blinder-Oaxaca decomposition of the performance gap between domestically owned and foreign-owned firms: endowment effects. Solid bars represent statistically significant factors.

same level of productivity if they had the same level of endowments in those factors. Thus policies to address constraints on those factors would help to close the foreign-domestic gap in business performance.

Industrial Clusters in Africa

Given that firm size is an overarching constraint for the vast majority of domestic enterprises in Africa, a natural question concerns what facilitates the growth of micro and small enterprises. Various studies have been conducted to address how the four factors—capital intensity, market access, managers' education, and access to finance—among others, facilitate or constrain growth of those enterprises. Another approach to the issue is to try to understand how those enterprises are coping with constraints on the ground, how the coping mechanisms work, and what their benefits and shortfalls are.

One promising mechanism that can facilitate growth for small African firms is the formation of industrial clusters. An industrial cluster is a geographic concentration of firms in the same or related industries. These natural agglomerations of micro and small enterprises are common in major cities in Africa. This study investigates how industrial clusters could help micro and small domestic enterprises to overcome their size constraints and improve both their sales performance and their access to new markets.

While the manufacturing base is considered weak in Africa because of the spotty presence of large, competitive domestic manufacturers, industrial clusters appear to provide pockets of vitality in Africa's private sector. To examine their success, this research project conducted a set of case studies of industrial clusters in five countries—Cameroon, Ghana, Kenya, Mauritius, and Rwanda—focusing on the role of spontaneously grown clusters in light manufacturing industries, such as textiles and garments, furniture, and metalwork and equipment. An in-depth study was also conducted in the Arusha furniture cluster in Tanzania.

A key finding of the research is that cluster-based micro and small enterprises are performing better—both in sales performance and ability to reach distant markets—than enterprises of the same size, in the same industries, and in the same cities, but outside the clusters (see figures 5 and 6). Decomposing the *cluster premium* on sales performance—the margin an enterprise gets in sales performance from being inside the cluster—shows that the higher capital intensity inside the cluster is the primary factor behind the cluster premium in sales performance. That is, agglomeration of enterprises leads to more capital accumulation inside the clusters.

Figure 5   Sales Performance in Light Manufacturing Clusters in Africa

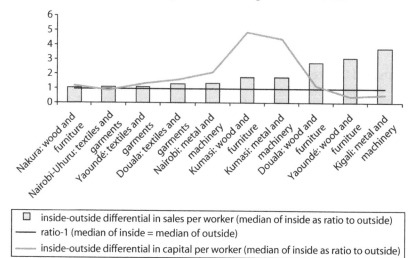

☐ inside-outside differential in sales per worker (median of inside as ratio to outside)
—— ratio-1 (median of inside = median of outside)
—— inside-outside differential in capital per worker (median of inside as ratio to outside)

Source: Bougna and Yoshino 2009, based on the data of micro and small enterprises inside the 10 light manufacturing clusters and their outside comparators collected as part of the original five-country case studies of industrial clusters.

The study also finds that the strength in numbers that comes from clustering has significant benefits for those businesses. There is strong empirical evidence to show that "joint action" by firms in the clusters, such as joint sales practices, help enterprises to penetrate distant markets.

Also, enterprises located inside the clusters have a higher probability of attracting new customers who come to shop where the clusters are. Another interesting observation from the case studies is that cluster-based enterprises are more likely to buy their inputs from other enterprises within the same cluster, while selling their products outside. The pattern supports the hypothesis that strong buyer-seller networks operate within clusters, while clusters facilitate access to external markets for outputs.

Growth Constraints for Survival Clusters

Naturally formed industrial clusters can mitigate some of the constraints that micro and small enterprises face in attaining access to capital and markets. The case studies show that accessibility to customers is the leading reason enterprises decide to locate within industrial clusters. An in-depth case study of the Arusha furniture cluster—comprising more than 200 carpentry workshops and outlets—finds that ethnicity facilitates the

Figure 6   Market Access Performance in Light Manufacturing Clusters in Africa

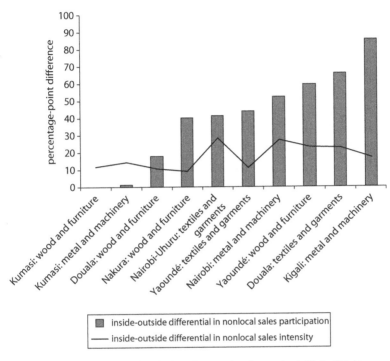

Source: Bougna and Yoshino 2009, based on the data of micro and small enterprises inside the 10 light manufacturing clusters and their outside comparators collected as part of the original five-country case studies of industrial clusters.
Note: Inside-outside percentage-point differential in participation and intensity of sales in nonlocal markets.

initial choice of location of new entrants as well as the market thickness of the particular location chosen.

However, cluster-based enterprises face another set of unique growth constraints. By the very nature of spontaneous agglomeration, new enterprises continue to flow to the clusters, seeking the profit opportunities and better access to markets available at such locations. The result can be intense competition within the clusters that leads to lower sales revenue, value added, and profitability in addition to increased congestion.

Space constraints often impede growth within clusters. Given inherent space constraints associated with industrial agglomeration, industrial clusters easily face land shortages and physical congestion. Data show that good performers in the clusters tend to seek alternative locations. However, the lack of alternative locations available for industrial activities in the same cities, generic infrastructure bottlenecks (particularly transport and power), and unclear zoning policies and their unpredictable changes limit firms' choice of location and constrain their mobility.

Another constraint is the lack of capability among cluster-based enterprises to innovate and invest to differentiate their products. While competition improves overall efficiency by weeding out inefficient enterprises, the inability of competing enterprises to invest and innovate because they lack access to finance and have poor managerial skills and knowledge inhibits competition from being translated into growth. The vast majority of naturally formed clusters of light manufacturing industries in Africa are still at the survival stage, where agglomeration leads to expansion of production by reproducing the same products, but not yet to quality improvements and product differentiation through innovation, as observed in more advanced innovation-oriented clusters elsewhere in the world. Product differentiation is an essential element for competitiveness and ultimately for sustained growth of the cluster.

Building Managerial Human Capital

Existing studies on industrial clusters in Africa point to the lack of managerial skills and knowledge among entrepreneurs running micro and small enterprises as a major constraint on innovation and growth in the clusters. It takes a certain level of education to attain the business acumen to upgrade product lines and improve production, quality management, marketing methods, and financial methods—improvements that allow industrial clusters to maintain profitability and grow in an environment of increasing internal competition. There are several cases in Africa in which enterprises managed by entrepreneurs with better knowledge in marketing and other managerial skills succeeded in "graduating" from survival-level clusters to more upscale formal industrial areas.

As part of this study, the team conducted pilot managerial skills training programs in two industrial clusters: one in Suame Magazine in Kumasi, Ghana, the other in Kariobangi Light Industries in Nairobi, Kenya. In each location, a group of randomly selected entrepreneurs within the cluster was given a three-week crash course on basic management skills and practices such as bookkeeping, marketing, business planning, and production management. The impact evaluation of the pilots showed that the training programs had a significant positive impact on the value added and gross profits of enterprises. Visible improvements were made in routine business practices such as record keeping, advertising, and maintaining an organized workplace, among participants of the training program after the training. For example, the net effect of the training was equivalent to about 160 percent growth in gross profits over one year both in Kariobangi and in Suame Magazine.

Implications for Policies

Raising survival-level industrial clusters to a more dynamic, innovating state will be an important avenue for fostering growth of micro and small enterprises and building a more viable domestic private sector. Existing spontaneously formed industrial clusters have the potential to be natural incubators for micro and small enterprises, but the constraints mentioned will prohibit this growth unless national efforts are undertaken to improve the investment climate and investments in human capital. Especially important are specific policies targeted to existing industrial clusters and the micro and small domestic enterprises within them.

Penetration into global markets outside of Africa continues to be a big challenge for micro and small enterprises. However, deeper regional economic integration and improved cross-border trade facilitation at the regional level provide a more immediate avenue for domestic entrepreneurs to form links with external markets. Policies can also provide an environment in which cluster-based micro and small enterprises can be better linked with larger enterprises that have access to global markets, including foreign-owned enterprises.

One of the most serious constraints on the investment climate in Africa is limited access to land and the lack of a sound policy framework to support market-oriented land allocation. This constraint limits the ability of enterprises to choose an optimal location, constraining the ability of informal micro and small enterprises to formalize their operations. For clusters to grow, they need to be supported by the process of urbanization in the economy, which would provide more possible locations for enterprises. Sound spatial planning policy, particularly urban planning at the local level, is needed. This includes optimal spatial allocation of infrastructure and other public goods, transparent and predictable zoning policy, and efforts to address negative externalities from agglomeration such as congestion and pollution.

Key elements that would help micro and small enterprises to build linkages with external markets are managerial education and skill development, as well as improved access to credit. Targeting clusters in managerial skill development programs may be effective for three reasons. First, managerial skill development programs that target only a subset of cluster-based entrepreneurs could be cost-effective because of spillover effects from those who receive the training to those who do not. Second, improved management leads to better profitability in industrial clusters, creating more jobs, particularly for young workers. Third, building managerial human capital within clusters not only makes enterprises more competitive but also induces them to join the formal sector. Managerial skill training in African clusters is one small but important step toward developing a strong indigenous private sector, as observed in other regions of the world.

CHAPTER 1

Introduction

While many African countries recognize the centrality of the private sector for economic growth and diversification, their domestic private sector is still small and thin. The goal of this study is to understand the constraints that domestic micro and small enterprises in Africa face in improving productivity and expanding their markets. The study focuses on how naturally formed industrial clusters could potentially mitigate those constraints and enhance their business performance. The study makes comprehensive quantitative inquiries about industrial clusters in Africa. It further lays out the advantages and challenges to clusters and the firms they house and presents the promising results of managerial training to cluster-based entrepreneurs.

This introductory chapter describes the private sector in Africa today to set the background for the study. It discusses the dualistic structure of the private sector in Africa, where a large number of micro and small enterprises, mostly indigenous domestic enterprises operating in an informal setting, coexist with a small number of large enterprises, often foreign-owned or former state-owned enterprises, generating a lion's share of private sector output in the economy. The chapter then presents a set of stylized facts about the performance gaps between domestically owned and foreign-owned enterprises.

Chapter 2 seeks to unbundle the factors behind the performance gaps between domestically owned and foreign-owned enterprises operating in Africa. In addition to the size of enterprises, it focuses on four other important factors: educational background of managers, access to finance, capital intensity, and access to nonlocal markets (national and export markets). The chapter unbundles the foreign-domestic productivity gap into those factors using pooled firm-level data collected by the World Bank Enterprise Surveys (WBESs) in 21 African countries. It also analyzes how productivity plays an important role in the foreign-domestic gap in access to nonlocal markets.

In an environment where size matters, micro and small enterprises face particularly severe challenges in overcoming numerous constraints. This report discusses how industrial clusters—natural, physical agglomerations of industrial and commercial activities—could help micro and small domestic enterprises to overcome these constraints by improving their productivity and market access. The conceptual framework of industrial clusters is presented in chapter 3. The subsequent two chapters (chapters 4 and 5) introduce findings from a set of case studies on industrial clusters in Africa. The discussion focuses specifically on naturally formed, spontaneously grown clusters of micro and small enterprises in light manufacturing industries, such as textiles and garments, furniture, and metalwork and equipment. Chapter 4 discusses how cluster-based enterprises perform better in both productivity and market access than their comparator enterprises outside the clusters. Chapter 5 discusses more dynamic aspects of clusters, including the choice of location of cluster-based enterprises and how market accessibility is an important factor for enterprises choosing to locate in a cluster.

The naturally formed industrial clusters in Africa face growth challenges, which is the topic of chapter 6. Those clusters are still largely at an early "survival" stage, where the formation of clusters simply increases the quantity of production, but does not necessarily improve the quality of product produced. Clusters in Africa are quite different from the more advanced, innovation-oriented clusters seen elsewhere in the world, where clustering generates innovation and enterprises compete by differentiating their products from those of their competitors. While competition improves the clusters' overall economic efficiency by weeding out inefficient enterprises, the lack of capacity to invest and innovate—resulting from inadequate access to finance and poor managerial skills and knowledge—is still a significant bottleneck to sustainable growth for enterprises in the clusters. Another growth bottleneck for survival-type clusters in Africa is the limited opportunity for cluster-based enterprises to improve their position by moving to an alternative location. Reducing these two bottlenecks to growth is crucial if industrial clusters are to evolve from survival into growth.

Existing studies have found that the lack of managerial skills among entrepreneurs running micro and small enterprises is a major constraint on innovation and growth in clusters, one of the two growth bottlenecks facing survival-type industrial clusters in Africa. As part of this study, pilot managerial skills training programs were conducted on an experimental basis in two industrial clusters in Africa. The programs covered marketing, accounting, and production management. Chapter 7 discusses the impacts of the training programs on business practices and business performance among entrepreneurs based in the clusters.

Chapter 8 concludes with a discussion of the policy implications of the empirical findings for facilitating the growth of micro and small enterprises within clusters.

Dualistic Structure of the Private Sector in Africa

The private sector is the engine of economic growth, stimulating entrepreneurship and innovation and promoting competition and productivity. Although foreign direct investment has been touted as an important avenue through which the private sector drives economic growth in developing countries, a national economy cannot grow unless there is a productive and profitable domestic private sector.

Evidence shows that Africa needs a stronger private sector to accelerate its economic growth.[1] Low volume and low efficiency in investment are two significant factors contributing to Africa's slow economic growth. Africa only has about half of the average investment efficiency of other developing regions. A little less than half of the growth gap between Africa and other developing regions can be attributed to slower accumulation of physical capital and the remainder to slower productivity growth (Ndulu and others 2007). The private sector is one area where larger productivity gains are needed in Africa.

Despite the fact that many African countries have developed private sector–based development strategies, Africa's formal private sector is still small, as reflected in the low rate of private investment. In the past five years the private investment rate in Africa was 13 percent of GDP, which is lower than in other regions with similarly low income levels, such as South Asia, which recorded a private investment rate of 22 percent of

GDP during the same period.[2] The public sector still occupies the lion's share of economic activity in Africa, not only in social services but also in productive sectors. In many countries, state-owned enterprises and parastatals continue to control a significant portion of production and services in the economy.

A poor investment climate with high risk and high transaction costs in doing business inhibits private sector growth in Africa. There are several reasons for the small size of Africa's private sector. First, relatively strong state interventions in the market, as well as excessive and inefficient regulations, have inhibited private sector growth. Second, private businesses face high transaction costs and high risks in an environment where market institutions are weak and infrastructure is poor. Overall, the cost of doing business is 20 to 40 percent higher in Africa than in other developing regions because of high regulatory costs, unsecured land property rights, inadequate and high-cost infrastructure, and ineffective judiciary systems. A poor investment climate and an underdeveloped financial sector are core reasons for Africa's limited export competitiveness and low foreign and domestic investment (World Bank 2009).

In the latest *Doing Business* report of the World Bank (2010), only eight Sub-Saharan African countries are in the top 100 of the 183 countries rated in the "ease-of-doing-business" index.[3] The rankings are based on each country's percentile ranking on 10 topics, including starting a business, construction permits, employing workers, access to credit, registering property, protecting investors, taxes, contract enforcement, trade across borders, and closing a business. Two-thirds of the low-income Sub-Saharan African countries are in the bottom quartile in the overall *Doing Business* ranking (see figure 1.1, panel a). For the most part, Sub-Saharan African countries measured poorly compared with countries in other regions (figure 1.1, panel b).

The poor investment climate is also connected to the presence of a large informal economy. As in other developing countries around the world, there are large numbers of informal enterprises in Africa. Although statistics are scarce, several case studies have shown the significant weight and rapid growth of this sector in terms of employment as well as economic growth for low-income segments of the population. Its contribution to GDP is growing rapidly as well (Fox and Gaal 2008).

The sparseness of the private sector base in Africa is reflected in its dual structure, which consists of a large number of small-scale domestic enterprises and a small number of large-scale foreign enterprises. On the one hand, a small number of large-scale enterprises, often owned by

Figure 1.1   *Doing Business* Indicators of Sub-Saharan Africa

a. Overall ranking, *Doing Business* indicators

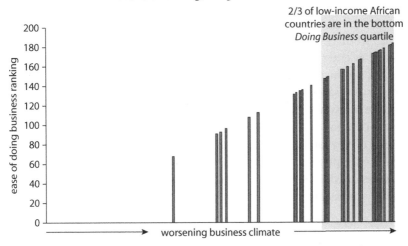

Source: World Bank 2010; Moss 2009.

b. Regional average of select indicators

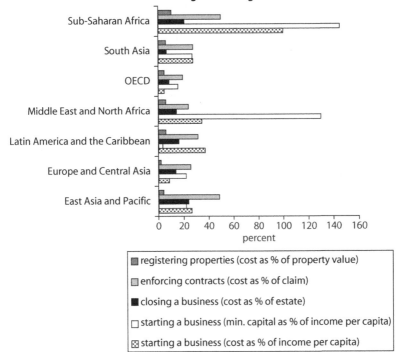

Source: World Bank 2010.

foreigners, dominate the formal private sector, generating the lion's share of commercial output in the economy. On the other hand, numerous micro and small enterprises, predominantly owned by local domestic entrepreneurs, operate in the informal part of the economy. Based on the WBES from 17 African countries, figure 1.2 shows that large enterprises, defined as enterprises with more than 100 workers, are very few in number, but produce a large share of total aggregated sales in the private sector.[4] At the same time, small enterprises are dominant in number, but produce a less aggregated amount than larger enterprises. Among enterprises operating in Africa, those owned by foreign nationals are spread relatively evenly among the various size groups. However, domestically owned enterprises, particularly those owned by ethnically African entrepreneurs or what one may call indigenous enterprises, are skewed toward smaller size, as judged by the number of workers (see figure 1.3).

Performance Gap between Domestically Owned and Foreign-Owned Enterprises in Africa

The dualistic nature of the private sector in Africa is reflected in the stark difference in productivity between average foreign-owned enterprises and average domestically owned firms, particularly those owned

Figure 1.2   Aggregate Sales and Number of Enterprises in Sub-Saharan Africa, by Size

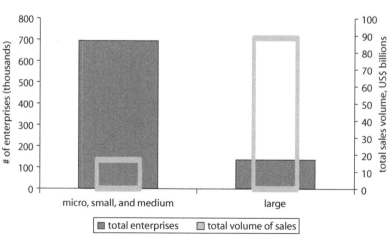

Source: Authors' estimation based on WBES data from 17 Sub-Saharan African countries, for which sample weights are available.

Figure 1.3   Size Distribution of Enterprises in Africa, by Nationality and Ethnicity of Owner

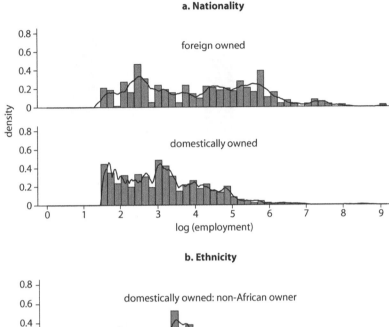

a. Nationality

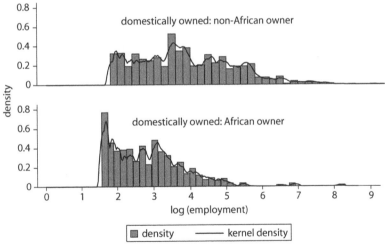

b. Ethnicity

Source: Authors' estimation based on WBES data from 17 Sub-Saharan African countries, for which sample weights are available.

by ethnically African entrepreneurs. Labor productivity of domestically owned enterprises, particularly ethnically African enterprises, measured by value added per worker, is significantly lower than that of foreign-owned enterprises (see figure 1.4).[5] A similar pattern is observed for sales per worker.

Figure 1.4   Foreign-Domestic Differences in Productivity and Growth in Africa

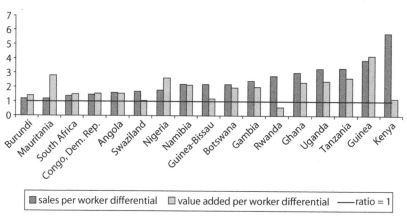

Source: Authors' estimation based on WBES data from 17 Sub-Saharan African countries, for which sample weights are available.
Note: PPP = purchasing power parity.

Figure 1.5   Foreign-Domestic Productivity Differential in Africa, by Country

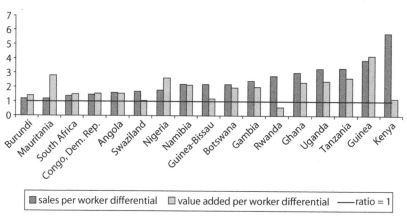

Source: Authors' estimation based on WBES data.

There are sizable variations in the performance of domestically owned and foreign-owned enterprises in African countries. The lagging performance of domestically owned enterprises, shown in figure 1.4, is based on the aggregation of all African countries in the current data set used for the study, and a few countries might be skewing the results. Figure 1.5 shows the current foreign-domestic productivity differential, calculated as the ratio of the median value added per worker among foreign-owned enterprises to the median among domestically owned enterprises. For sales per worker, domestically owned enterprises have lower productivity than foreign-owned enterprises in all countries in the data set. For value added per worker, domestically owned enterprises have lower productivity than foreign-owned enterprises in all countries except Rwanda. Thus the positive foreign-domestic productivity differential is consistent across all countries in the data set.

There are also significant variations among different sectors with regard to the foreign-domestic gap in business performance, with a larger gap observed among capital-intensive sectors. Figure 1.6 shows the foreign-domestic gap by sector. The mineral sector, for example, shows large differentials between domestically owned and foreign-owned enterprises. Technology-intensive and capital-intensive manufacturing sectors, such as electronics, chemicals, and machinery, also have large gaps. The gaps are relatively modest for light manufacturing, such as textiles and garments, and other manufacturing, such as furniture. Services tend to have smaller performance gaps. Therefore, the capital intensity of sectors seems to be correlated with the sector-specific productivity differential between foreign and domestic enterprises.

In fact, foreign-owned enterprises and large domestically owned enterprises are, on average, more capital intensive than smaller, domestically owned enterprises. The larger productivity gaps in more capital-intensive sectors, as shown in figure 1.6, are corroborated by a pattern of foreign-owned enterprises having higher capital-labor ratios; that is, they are more capital intensive than domestically owned enterprises (see figure 1.7). Capital intensity also varies significantly by size

Figure 1.6   Foreign-Domestic Productivity Differential in Africa, by Sector

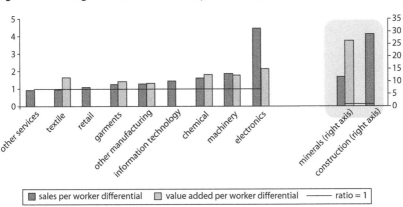

Source: Authors' estimation based on WBES data.

Figure 1.7   Capital-Labor Ratio in Africa, by Nationality, Size, and Sector

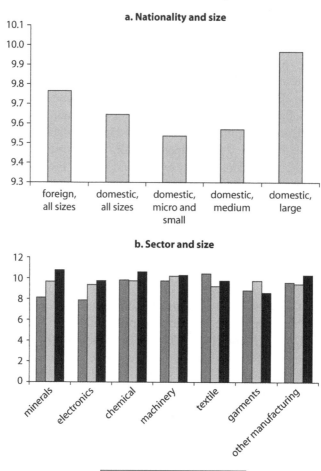

Source: Authors' estimation based on WBES data.

of enterprise. Larger enterprises are much more capital intensive than small enterprises. Furthermore, capital-intensive sectors appear to have sharper differences in the capital-labor ratio among small, medium, and large enterprises.[6]

A foreign-domestic gap is also found in the degree of penetration in geographically larger sales markets such as national and export markets, with smaller domestic enterprises having much less access to such markets than foreign-owned and large domestically owned enterprises.

Figure 1.8 shows that small domestic enterprises predominantly serve only local markets within the same neighborhood or city. However, within domestically owned enterprises, there is a significant variation among size groups. For 91 percent of small domestic enterprises, the principal market is local. Large domestic enterprises have almost the same level of market penetration as foreign enterprises. For approximately half of the large domestic enterprises, the principal market is either national or international as opposed to local.

Foreign-owned enterprises and larger domestically owned enterprises throughout the world have an advantage over smaller domestically owned enterprises in penetrating export markets. Because they are technologically superior and have enhanced access to international commercial networks, foreign-owned enterprises tend to be more productive and have better access to geographically wider markets than do domestically owned enterprises. This is true in most countries in the world and therefore not unique to Africa. Similarly, larger firms, on average, have better access to export markets because fixed costs make it relatively difficult for small enterprises to enter those markets. However, micro and small enterprises and domestically owned enterprises in Africa appear to be more constrained from participating in export markets than similar enterprises in other regions (see figure 1.9).

Figure 1.8   Rate of Participation in Local, National, and International Sales Markets in Africa, by Nationality and Size

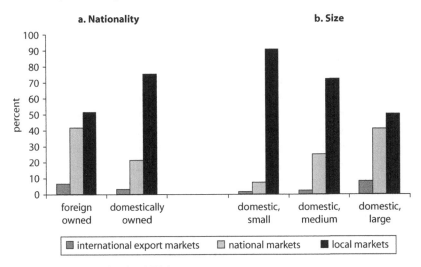

Source: Authors' estimation based on WBES data.

Figure 1.9   Rate of Participation in Export Markets among Domestically Owned Enterprises and Micro and Small Enterprises, by Country

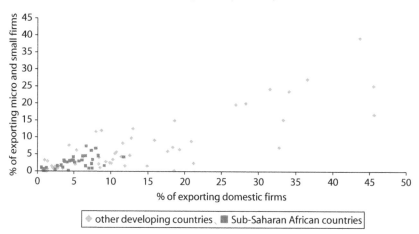

Source: Authors' estimation based on WBES data.

Size differences between domestically owned and foreign-owned enterprises may explain a large part of the observed gap in performance. As shown in figure 1.10, foreign-owned enterprises tend to be larger and more productive than domestic enterprises. The correlation between firm size and performance in Africa has been widely documented in the literature. A few studies have shown the presence of economies of scale in manufacturing sectors, where larger firms tend to be more productive.

There is also less growth among small enterprises in Africa. Several studies that have examined patterns of firm turnover in Sub-Saharan Africa consistently report higher turnover rates among smaller firms (for example, Harding, Söderbom, and Teal 2004). While findings on the relationship between size and firm growth are mixed, Sleuwaegen and Goedhuys (2002) find strong evidence of positive effects of firm age and size on growth, implying that the concavity in firm growth over time (firm age) is less pronounced for larger firms. Ramachandran, Gelb, and Shah (2009) find that firms owned by ethnic minority entrepreneurs, such as those of Asian or European descent, start out larger and grow significantly faster than indigenously owned firms, largely as a result of economies of scale. At the same time, the data robustly demonstrate that, among firms owned by indigenous African entrepreneurs, those with

Figure 1.10   Size and Productivity of Domestic and Foreign Enterprises in Africa

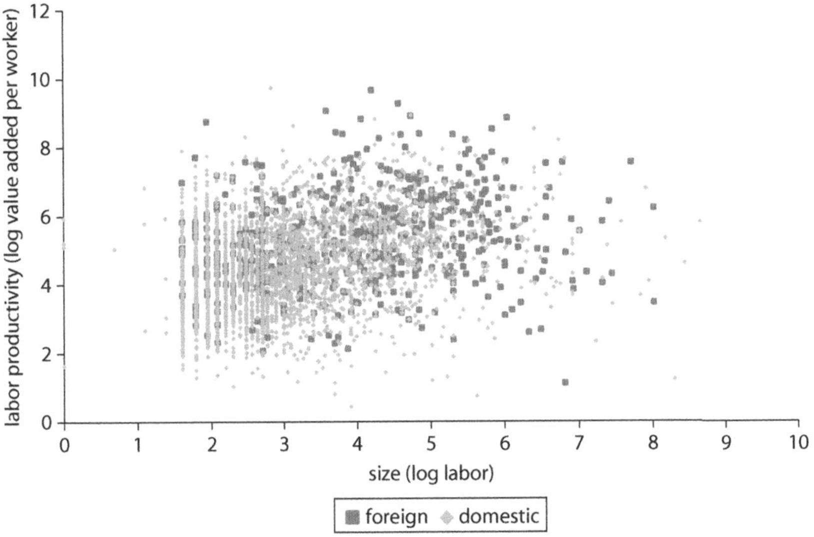

Source: Authors' estimation based on WBES data.

university-educated owners show higher growth rates. In Tanzania, for example, the average start-up size for enterprises owned by ethnic minorities was about 60 employees; however, the start-up size for domestic firms was just under 20 employees. In most African countries, minority-owned enterprises started at a size two to three times larger than domestic indigenous enterprises (Ramachandran, Gelb, and Shah 2009). Also, firms that start small tend to stay small, and, in many instances, a substantial gap develops over time between the size of indigenous and minority-owned firms.

Notes

1. Throughout the report, Africa indicates Sub-Saharan Africa only.
2. Based on gross fixed capital formation in 2009 as a percentage of GDP (World Development Indicators as of October 2010).
3. Those are four low-income countries, namely Rwanda (67), Zambia (90), Ghana (92), and Kenya (95). In addition to those, four middle-income African countries are in the top 100, namely Mauritius (17), South Africa (34), Botswana (45), and Namibia (66).

4. Those 17 countries are Angola, Botswana, Burundi, the Democratic Republic of Congo, The Gambia, Ghana, Guinea, Guinea-Bissau, Kenya, Mauritania, Namibia, Nigeria, Rwanda, South Africa, Swaziland, Tanzania, and Uganda. Burkina Faso, Cameroon, Cape Verde, and Ethiopia, which are included in the analysis in chapter 2, are omitted from the analysis in this chapter due to the absence of sampling weights.

5. Foreign ownership of an enterprise is determined by the presence of foreign-owned shares in the enterprise.

6. This pattern is understandable given the fact that the size categories are based on the number of workers so that more capital-intensive sectors should show higher jumps in the capital-labor ratio as the number of workers moves from one level to the next.

References

Fox, M. Louise, and Melissa Sekkel Gaal. 2008. *Working out of Poverty: Job Creation and the Quality of Growth in Africa*. Washington, DC: World Bank.

Harding Alan, Måns Söderbom, and Francis Teal. 2004. "Survival and Success among African Manufacturing Firms." CSAE Working Paper Series 2004-05, Centre for the Study of African Economies, University of Oxford.

Moss, Todd. 2009. "A Question for Raj Shah: How to Bring Order to U.S. Support for Business Climate Reforms?" *Global Development: Views from the Center (Blog)*. Center for Global Development. http://blogs.cgdev.org/globaldevelopment/ 2009/11/a-question-for-raj-shah-how-to-bring-order-to-u-s-support-for-business-climate-reforms.php

Ndulu, Benno J., Lopamudra Chakraborti, Lebahang Lijane, Vijaya Ramachandran, and Jerome Wolgin. 2007. *Challenges of African Growth: Opportunities, Constraints, and Strategic Directions*. Washington, DC: World Bank.

Ramachandran, Vijaya, Alan Gelb, and Manju Shah. 2009. *Africa's Private Sector: What's Wrong with the Business Environment and What to Do about It*. Washington, DC: Center for Global Development.

Sleuwaegen, L. and Micheline Goedhuys. 2002. "Growth of firms in developing countries, evidence from Côte d'Ivoire." *Journal of Development Economics* 68: 117–135

World Bank. 2009. "Enhancing Growth and Reducing Poverty in a Volatile World: A Progress Report on the Africa Action Plan." World Bank, Washington, DC (September 2).

———. 2010. *Doing Business 2010*. Washington, DC: World Bank.

CHAPTER 2

Unbundling Foreign-Domestic Performance Gaps in Africa's Private Sector

While the stark difference in size may explain a large part of the performance gap between domestically owned and foreign-owned enterprises in Africa, better performance in terms of productivity, sales performance, and market expansion is essential for individual enterprises to grow. It is therefore important to identify factors that improve business performance among domestic enterprises, particularly locally owned micro and small enterprises.

This chapter quantitatively unbundles and analyzes the factors that contribute to the gap in business performance among domestic African enterprises. The analysis was conducted at the regional level using firm-level survey data collected from the World Bank Enterprise Surveys (WBESs) in a wide range of countries in Africa (see box 2.1 for a brief description of WBESs). A set of econometric analyses was conducted on labor productivity, measured by sales per worker and value added per worker, using WBES data from 21 Sub-Saharan African countries: Angola, Botswana, Burkina Faso, Burundi, Cameroon, Cape Verde, the Democratic Republic of Congo, Ethiopia, The Gambia, Ghana, Guinea, Guinea-Bissau, Kenya, Mauritania, Namibia, Nigeria, Rwanda, South Africa, Swaziland, Tanzania, and Uganda.[1] The data for each country include not only manufacturing sectors but also several services sectors such as retail and construction.[2]

Box 2.1

World Bank Enterprise Surveys

The WBES present the enterprise data that the World Bank Group has been collecting from a large number of countries to measure the business performance of enterprises operating in individual countries as well as objective and subjective data on various aspects of the business environment, as experienced by individual enterprises. The data are used to prepare the investment climate assessment reports the Bank produces for individual countries. The assessment is updated periodically and at a government's request. The data are collected through surveys that ask a common set of questions in all countries. The survey is completed by managing directors, accountants, human resource managers, and other enterprise staff. The manufacturing sector is covered in all countries, while the services sector (tourism, transport, construction, retail, and so on) is covered in most countries. Micro enterprises are also covered based on a simplified questionnaire. The firms are selected by simple random sampling or random stratified sampling that controls for size, subsector, and geographic distribution, based on the company registration records or manufacturing census information available from the government. More than 80 countries have been surveyed since the program began in 2002. Surveys are performed approximately every three years. The most recent data were collected in 2007. The WBES also produces enterprise notes and research papers on informality, natural resources, property rights, consumer behavior, labor regulation, crime and security, and other topics.

Source: www.enterprisesurveys.org.

The analysis of the gap in labor productivity, measured by value added per worker and sales per worker, is complemented by an analysis of the foreign-domestic gap in firm participation in larger sales markets using the same data set. This takes into account not only whether enterprises export, but also whether they participate in markets beyond local markets, including both national domestic markets and international export markets. For micro and small enterprises, expanding beyond their local community to markets elsewhere in the country is one of the most immediate challenges.

Productivity Gap

The literature on the private sector in Africa points to two factors that are significant in explaining the performance gap for micro and small enterprises in Africa: access to finance and manager's educational background.

Empirical work on African firms, such as Ramachandran, Gelb, and Shah (2009), suggests that the education level of managers and access to finance are the two most significant constraints on indigenous African firms, which constitute the bulk of micro and small enterprises in Africa. This work highlights the significant role of informal social networks that increase the flow of information among indigenous firms, reduce search costs, build trust relationships, and reduce transaction costs. In an environment where market institutions are weak, such networks may facilitate access to finance. Managers' educational background not only signals their entrepreneurial ability, but also helps to build social networks instrumental for running a successful business.

The lack of access to finance is one of the most frequently cited constraints on the investment climate in Africa. African financial systems are shallow, and this shallowness is related to low income. Only about 20 percent of African adults have an account at a formal or semiformal financial institution. The ratio of private credit to GDP averages 18 percent in Africa, compared with 30 percent in South Asia and 107 percent in high-income countries. Africa is also the continent with the largest risk of capital flight. African banks have high interest rates for reasons related to profitability and operating costs. Weaker property rights cause banks to charge high interest rates and to spend more administrative resources on credit appraisal and monitoring (Honohan and Beck 2007).

In almost all of the investment climate assessments for individual African countries that the World Bank conducts regularly, access to finance is raised as a major constraint. The weak financial sector in Africa raises the costs of securing financial capital through formal channels. Collateral requirements are often cited as the primary reason for enterprises not to apply for a loan. Some entrepreneurs are better able to mobilize financial resources through their own internal networks based on ethnicity. Trade credits are important ways of obtaining external financing, and the ability to obtain trade credits depends on the trust between buyers and suppliers that is built through repeated transactions.

The educational background of entrepreneurs, particularly those with higher education, contributes to business performance in several ways. Higher education facilitates the acquisition of both technical knowledge and entrepreneurial vision for managing a business and marketing products and services. At the same time, completion of a university degree provides a credential that attests to the person's general ability to succeed in business, which then facilitates his or her access to financial and other services as well as to buyers and sellers. The university degree may enable access to a network of other business professionals that is useful for success of the business. Ramachandran, Gelb, and Shah (2009) find that indigenous African entrepreneurs with a university education tend to start their business as a larger enterprise and that these enterprises remain larger than those of owners without a university education.

In addition to these two variables, several other factors need to be considered in analyzing the performance gap between foreign and domestic enterprises in Africa, one being capital intensity of production. Capital intensity of production is the measure of a firm's use of physical capital, such as machinery and equipment, relative to labor. More use of machinery and equipment per worker increases output per worker because machinery and equipment replace part of the manual labor of workers. Capital intensity also corresponds to the level of technology in production. Therefore, more intensive use of capital may also indicate that an enterprise is producing a higher-quality product. Access to finance affects the investment patterns of enterprises and thus their ability to obtain physical capital. Limited access to finance among micro and small enterprises in Africa constrains their investment in physical capital. In addition, market risks discourage them from investing in new assets. Gunning and Mengistae (2001) argue that investments in African manufacturing have been held back by high risk rather than low returns on investment.

Access to markets beyond local markets is another critical factor that facilitates higher productivity at the enterprise level, regardless of whether the larger market is national or international. Access to larger distant markets increases the volume of sales and, hence, raises productivity by creating economies of scale; it also provides incentives to expand production capacity. Also, as is discussed in the various studies that have looked at the relationship between productivity and exporting, enterprises increase productivity by exporting, gaining new knowledge and skills from serving overseas customers who have more diversified tastes than domestic customers, and from competing with a larger number of producers. This is often called the *learning-by-exporting* hypothesis.[3] A similar story applies to national domestic markets, where enterprises face potentially more competitors than in local markets and more diversified tastes among customers, particularly among micro and small enterprises (see figure 2.1).

The following section analyzes the foreign-domestic gap in labor productivity in two ways. First, it looks at how much domestic or foreign ownership explains the level of productivity of individual enterprises. Second, it systematically decomposes the foreign-domestic productivity gap into the following factors: access to finance, education level, market access, capital intensity, and size.

Figure 2.1   Number of Competitors, by Size of Enterprise and Type of Principal Sales Market

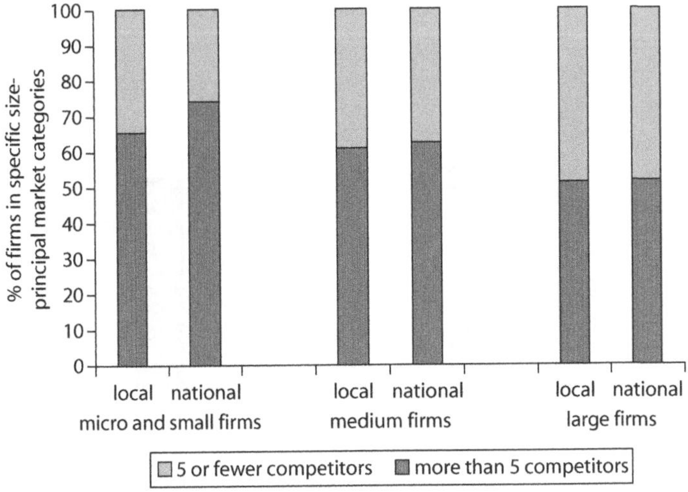

Source: Authors' estimation based on WBES data.

Effect of Domestic Ownership on Productivity

A series of regression analyses is conducted to see how the four factors—access to finance, manager's education level, market access, and capital intensity—together with size explain the existing foreign-domestic productivity gap by looking at how productivity is attributed to whether enterprises are domestically owned or foreign owned (*domestic ownership effect*) and how such attribution changes in the presence of the other factors. This is done by sequentially introducing each of these four factors in the regression on labor productivity and seeing how each individually reduces the negative effect of domestic ownership on productivity, as represented in the negative coefficient on domestic ownership in the regression.[4] The domestic ownership effect is expected to decrease gradually as other factors are introduced.[5] Instrumental variables are used to address the endogeneity problem with some factors, such as access to finance and sales to nonlocal markets, vis-à-vis the dependent variables, namely, sales performance and productivity.[6] This exercise is repeated in order to determine how size affects the way those factors contribute to the productivity gap.

Figure 2.2 demonstrates the declining magnitude of the negative domestic ownership effect on labor productivity (value added per worker and sales per worker).[7] The domestic ownership effect is large initially when taking only countries and industries into account, and this

Figure 2.2   Size of Domestic Ownership Effect on Business Performance: Percent Marginal Effect from Instrumental Variables Estimation

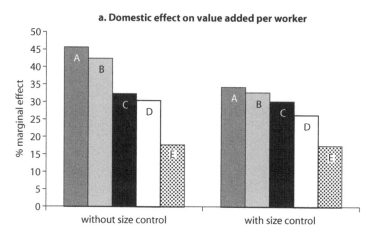

a. Domestic effect on value added per worker

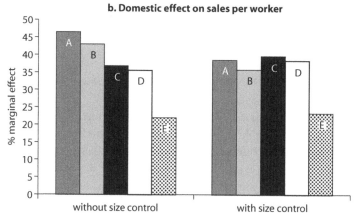

b. Domestic effect on sales per worker

Source: Feng, Mengistae, and Yoshino 2009.
Note: A = country and industry dummies; B = A plus manager's education; C = B plus access to formal finance; D = C plus capital intensity; E = D plus sales to nonlocal markets. Figures are shown in absolute values.

is also true when controlling for size. But it gradually shrinks as other factors are introduced.

Manager's education matters. Entrepreneurs typically become engaged in business after completing some level of formal education. Consistent with the findings from existing studies, the manager's education level is found to have an effect on the gap in labor productivity. The data show fewer domestic local entrepreneurs with postsecondary education than foreign entrepreneurs. Among domestic enterprises, 44 percent of managers have postsecondary education and only 26 percent have university education, compared with 78 and 48 percent of foreign entrepreneurs, respectively. The size of the domestic ownership effect decreases more if managers have university or other postsecondary education.

Access to finance leads to a sizable reduction in the domestic ownership effect when size is not controlled for. As entrepreneurs start up their business, they must secure financial capital. Several studies have documented that domestic enterprises have less access to formal finance than foreign enterprises. According to the WBES data used here, only 19 percent of domestic enterprises obtain formal financing. A relatively large reduction in the domestic ownership effect is observed when access to formal finance is captured in the regression without controlling for size. This pattern is clearly observed both in value added per worker and in sales per worker when size is not controlled for.

Access to physical capital further weakens the domestic ownership effect. Controlling for capital intensity, measured by capital per worker, further reduces the magnitude of the domestic ownership effect. This reduction occurs because access to finance allows firms to obtain more and better physical capital. In fact, once capital intensity is introduced, access to finance has a smaller effect on productivity.

The domestic ownership effect declines substantially as a result of participation in nonlocal markets. With a higher level of physical capital, enterprises can produce better-quality products, diversify their product lines, or both. The level of productivity also improves with increased physical capital. Improved productivity and the development of new product lines could enable firms to expand their market space and sell their products outside of local markets, that is, in *nonlocal markets*, first to national markets and then to international export markets. This would further reduce the magnitude of the domestic ownership effect. The reduction in the domestic ownership effect, both on productivity and sales performance, is substantial once participation in nonlocal markets is controlled for.

The size factor explains a significant part of the domestic ownership effect and weakens its overall magnitude. This effect is particularly evident in the case of value added, but it also applies to sales performance, both of which are influenced by enterprise size. For example, a large enterprise faces fewer constraints in obtaining loans from a bank and is better able to expand its product markets.

When size is controlled, the coefficient for access to finance is not even statistically significant. However, the sharp drop in the domestic ownership effect from participation in nonlocal markets for sales remains significant, even when controlling for size. While access to finance becomes muted once size is controlled for, participation in nonlocal markets continues to have a pronounced impact. This suggests that an implicit factor unique to foreign enterprises facilitates their market expansion.

Unbundling the Foreign-Domestic Performance Gap

Next, an attempt is made to disentangle the foreign-domestic productivity gap more explicitly by using the Blinder-Oaxaca decomposition technique to decompose quantitatively the factors that contribute to the difference in labor productivity between domestic and foreign enterprises (Jann 2008). This decomposition technique allows us to identify systematically which factors contribute to the gap more significantly than others. A unique feature of this method is that it distinguishes among (a) effects that contribute to the productivity gap because they differ in quantity endowments of the factors between domestic and foreign groups (*endowment effects*); (b) effects that bias how those factors affect productivity differently between the two groups (*coefficient effects*), resulting in either strengthening or weakening the endowment effects, depending on their sign; and (c) the interactions between those two types of effects (*interaction effects*). See box 2.2 for further details.

Box 2.2

Blinder-Oaxaca Decomposition

Suppose we run linear regression on two separate samples, one domestic and another foreign; we can express the predicted differential in Y value between foreign and domestic enterprises as follows:

$$Y^F - Y^D = (X^F * \beta^F) - (X^D * \beta^D). \tag{1}$$

We can then express the predicted differential as follows:

$$Y^F - Y^D = [(X^F - X^D) * \beta^D] + [X^D * (\beta^F - \beta^D)] + [(X^F - X^D) * (\beta^F - \beta^D)]. \tag{2}$$

The term in the first square brackets of equation 2 represents the endowment effect due to the difference in X between the two groups. The term in the second square brackets represents the coefficient effects due to deviation of β between the two groups. This is due to differences in slope. The term in the third square brackets is the interaction between the difference in endowments and the difference in coefficients.

Source: O'Donnell and others 2008.

Overall, the foreign-domestic productivity gap exists because domestically owned enterprises are simply less endowed than foreign-owned enterprises in the key factors and not because those factors have any biasing effect against domestically owned enterprises. As shown in figures 2.3 and 2.4, the total combined endowment effect is statistically significant, but both coefficient and interaction effects are statistically insignificant. The pattern is the same for both value added per worker and sales per worker. This implies that addressing the low level of endowments among domestically owned enterprises would allow them to reduce the productivity gap with regard to foreign-owned enterprises. This is an encouraging finding because it implies that the return to investment in those key factors is the same for domestically owned and foreign-owned enterprises.

Participation in nonlocal markets has the largest endowment effect on the foreign-domestic productivity gap, followed by capital intensity and manager's education. Among individual factors, nonlocal market participation shows the largest and most significant endowment effect among the four factors. This is consistent with the result in which participation in nonlocal markets substantially reduces the effect

Figure 2.3   Decomposition of Domestic Ownership Effect on Value Added per Worker

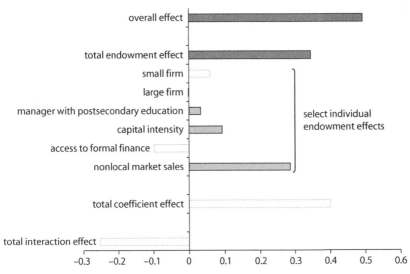

Source: Feng, Mengistae, and Yoshino 2009.
Note: Solid bars represent statistically significant factors. Country and industry effects as well as a constant are included in the analysis, but not reported in this figure.

Figure 2.4   Decomposition of Domestic Ownership Effect on Sales per Worker

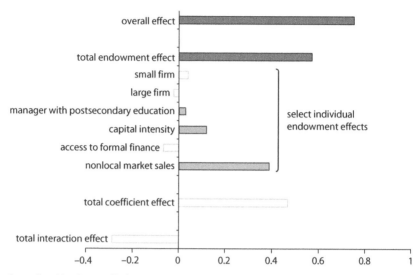

Source: Feng, Mengistae, and Yoshino 2009.
Note: Solid bars represent statistically significant factors. Country and industry effects as well as a constant are included in the analysis, but not reported in this figure.

of domestic ownership. Capital intensity and manager's education also have significant endowment effects. Again, the pattern corresponds to relatively visible reductions in the domestic ownership effect when controlling for those two factors. Access to formal finance is not significant when size is taken into account. This is consistent with the finding that the inclusion of size softens other factors.

Market Access: Participation in Nonlocal Markets

One of the key findings from analysis of the foreign-domestic productivity gap is that participation in nonlocal markets significantly helps domestically owned enterprises to reduce their productivity gap with foreign-owned enterprises. In fact, the ability of an enterprise to participate in spatially diversified markets is an important aspect of business performance. As shown in chapter 1, a much smaller proportion of domestic enterprises than foreign enterprises sell their products to nonlocal markets in Africa—that is, either national or international export markets. Among foreign enterprises in the study data, 49 percent sell mainly to markets outside their locality, and 7 percent sell mainly to other countries. In contrast, much smaller numbers of domestic enterprises sell their products outside their own city; three-quarters of them sell mainly to local markets in the same city.

As widely discussed in the literature on firm-level participation in exports, more productive firms are more likely to export and to export more intensively than less productive firms. Low productivity limits the ability of domestic enterprises to expand from local markets in the same neighborhood or city to national and international markets. There is a rich literature on productivity and firm-level export performance. Many studies have sought to identify the empirical correlation between productivity and export performance using firm-level micro data from both developed and developing countries.[8] The presence of fixed costs to entering a larger market requires a sufficiently high level of productivity for firms to be profitable upon entry, whether the larger market is national or international.[9]

The empirical relationship between productivity and export performance for African manufacturing firms is also well documented. For example, Mengistae and Pattillo (2004) use panel data on the manufacturing sector in three African countries (Ethiopia, Ghana, and Kenya) and estimate a significantly higher level of productivity among firms selling for export compared with firms selling only domestically.

Foreign-owned enterprises do better at exporting in Africa. Some studies have found foreign ownership to be statistically significant in firm-level export performance in the African manufacturing sector, including Rankin, Söderbom, and Teal (2006). Yoshino (2008) finds that foreign ownership is particularly relevant for exporting to global markets outside of Africa, as opposed to regional markets, allowing firms to export even when there are behind-the-border domestic business constraints. Trade facilitation effects from foreign ownership seem to surpass the domestic constraints facing firms. However, foreign ownership is less significant for regional trade within Africa, where relatively more domestic enterprises participate.

There are several reasons why the share of foreign ownership matters, in particular for global exports. First, foreign direct investment brings skills and technologies from source countries that are otherwise not available domestically. Such skills and technologies help to improve the physical productivity of firms (*productivity effects*). Another reason is that firms with foreign ownership are more likely to have access to established overseas business networks and marketing channels or to have their own cross-border corporate networks and channels, including with the country of their parent company, which facilitates their exporting activities (*network effects*).

Access to markets may be delineated along ethnic lines due to diaspora network effects as well. A body of literature examines how ethnic networks or communities help to facilitate exchange, particularly in contexts where formal institutions are lacking (for example, Greif 1993; Rauch and Trindade 2002; Biggs and Shah 2006). Differences in network effects between ethnically African and non-African groups may contribute to differences in market access. Nonindigenous social networks may have better access to markets as diaspora ties link entrepreneurs to overseas markets. There is some evidence for strong trade flows between immigrants and their country of origin and between entrepreneurs of the same ethnic origin.[10] Diaspora networks also connect entrepreneurs from the same ethnic group domestically among different cities as well as regionally among different countries in the same subregion.

Quantifying the Domestic Ownership Effect on Participation in Nonlocal Markets

The quantitative analysis using the WBES data is extended to analyze whether and how much the negative domestic ownership effect influences the scope for expanding markets among African enterprises. We are particularly interested in investigating the sequential expansion of market space from local to national (selling domestically but countrywide) and to international (exporting). For this reason, we use the ordered categorical variable in the WBES data, which indicates the principal market for an enterprise among those three market levels. The vast majority of studies have looked at firms' performance in exporting, including whether or not they export (export participation), how much they export (export intensity), and where they export to (geographic orientation). However, for domestic enterprises in Africa, the majority of which are small and less productive than foreign enterprises, it is important to capture their ability to expand beyond the local level, even within domestic markets.

The positive foreign ownership factor and the negative indigenous African ownership factor are both statistically significant, but they become weaker or insignificant once productivity is taken into account. Table 2.1 shows the results of the econometric analysis using an ordered probit model of the principal sales market for enterprises, coded as 0 for local market, 1 for national market, and 2 for international market. Foreign ownership is positive and significant for all three models, which

Table 2.1   Ordered Probit Estimation Results for Principal Market of Enterprises
dependent variable = principal sales market

Independent variable	Ordered probit without productivity (1)	Ordered probit with productivity (2)	Instrumental variable ordered probit with productivity (3)
Total factor productivity	n.a.	0.101***	0.129***
Foreign ownership (dummy)	0.227***	0.185**	0.186**
African indigenous ownership (dummy)	−0.106*	0.0809	0.0748
Small enterprise (dummy)	−0.396***	−0.314***	−0.288***
Large enterprise (dummy)	0.431***	0.315***	0.285***
Age of firm (log)	0.0594**	0.0579**	0.0509*
Manager received higher education (dummy)	0.191***	0.171***	0.165***
Private ownership (dummy)	0.105*	0.0618	0.0574
Access to credit is a concern (1–5 rank)	−0.0606	−0.0336	−0.0316
ISO certified (dummy)	0.256***	0.211***	0.207***
Located in zone (dummy)	0.196***	0.192***	0.182***
Number of observations	3,277	3,267	3,267

Source: Chan 2009.
Note: Country and sector dummies are included, but not reported. The ordered probit model on principal sales market for enterprises, is coded as 0 for local market, 1 for national market, and 2 for international market.
n.a. = not applicable.
*** $p < 0.01$.
** $p < 0.05$.
* $p < 0.10$.

means that the negative domestic ownership effect on market expansion is strong and robust. The size of the coefficient is smaller when the productivity level is taken into account. Similarly, the dummy variable for being owned by ethnically indigenous Africans is negative and significant initially. However, the effect disappears once productivity is taken into account. As there may be potential issues with the endogeneity of firm productivity and market participation, firm-specific historical sales are used as the instrument for productivity. The pattern appears to be robust. Age, educational background of managers, size factors, and certification under international product standards—for example, ISO (International Organization for Standardization) certification—are also significant for all specifications, consistent with the empirical literature on firm-level export behavior.

Notes

1. Those countries are selected based purely on the availability of data after 2005. Countries with surveys conducted in 2005 or earlier were not included in this analysis due to differences in the survey instruments.

2. The service sector was included only for the analysis of sales per worker because information on material costs, which is necessary to compute value added, is not available for the service sector in WBESs.

3. As discussed later in the chapter, another hypothesis is that only productive enterprises choose to participate in export markets (*self-selection hypothesis*) given the fixed costs in exporting.

4. This is the negative coefficient of the dummy variable of having domestic African owners (by nationality) in the regression models.

5. The order of introducing those factors is designed along the sequence of possible actions entrepreneurs take in initiating a business, starting production, and marketing their products.

6. Instruments used for the regression are female ownership, initial size (number of employees when an enterprise was established), and an indicator showing how an enterprise perceives functioning trade-related institutions as more problematic than general business-related market institutions (as reflected in functioning legal institutions). Female ownership and initial size are both predetermined but are empirically related with how enterprises manage to obtain formal financing services. Female entrepreneurs face more difficulty in obtaining credit from formal financial institutions. If enterprises started as large enterprises, they should have more opportunities to obtain formal financing and to develop larger markets than small enterprises. The third indicator is correlated with enterprises' participation in nonlocal markets, but not their productivity. Productive enterprises tend to be affected by poorly functioning trade-related institutions and general market institutions, such as the judicial system. But only enterprises with the ability to expand market space to the national and international levels are affected by the functioning of trade-related institutions.

7. The complete coefficient estimate results are presented in appendix 1. The negative effects are shown in absolute values.

8. In the dynamic context, there are two lines of argument in the literature on how productivity and export performance influence each other. First, some studies argue that firm-level productivity matters in firms' decisions to export because the presence of sunk costs associated with exporting allows only productive firms to participate in export markets (for example, Roberts and Tybout 1997). This is often called the "self-selection hypothesis" because firms self-select to participate in exporting. Another line of argument is that the reason for the positive relationship between firm-level productivity and export performance is that firms can raise their productivity through

exports, acquiring foreign technologies and strengthening their competitiveness by exposing themselves to tougher competition in foreign markets (the "learning-by-exporting" hypothesis). Bigsten and others (2004) observe the learning-by-exporting effect among African manufacturing firms.

9. Other empirical papers on firm-level export performance for manufacturing firms in Africa include Soderböm and Teal (2002) and Milner and Tandrayen (2004).

10. Dunlevy (2004, 2006), Rauch and Trindade (2002), and Rauch (2001a, 2001b). For example, members of the Ethiopian diaspora in the United States are investing in their home country to start apparel exports to the United States under the African Growth and Opportunity Act.

References

A. T. Kearney. 2009. The Shifting Geography of Offshoring: The 2009 A. T. Kearney Global Services Index. Available online at www.atkearney.com

Biggs, Tyler, and Manju Shah. 2006. "African SMEs, Networks, and Manufacturing Performance." *Journal of Banking and Finance* 30 (11): 3043–66.

Bigsten, Arne, Paul Collier, Stefan Dercon, Marcel Fafchamps, Bernard Gauthier, Jan W. Gunning, Abena Oduro, Remco Oostedorp, Catherine Pattillo, Måns Soderböm, Francis Teal, and Albert Zeufeck. 2004. "Do African Manufacturing Firms Learn from Exporting?" *Journal of Development Studies* 40 (3): 115–41.

Chan, Rosanna C. 2009. "Drivers of Market Participation: Does Being Indigenous Matter?" Analytical background note prepared for the study.

Dongier, Phillipe, and Randeep Sudom. 2009. "Realizing the Opportunities Presented by the Global Trade in IT-Based Services." In *Information and Communications in Development 2009: Extending Reach and Increasing Impact*, 103-22. Washington, DC: World Bank.

Dunlevy, James A. 2004. "Interpersonal Networks in International Trade: Evidence on the Role of Immigrants in Promoting Exports from the American States." Working Paper, Miami University, Oxford, OH.

———. 2006. "The Influence of Corruption and Language on the Pro-Trade Effect of Immigrants: Evidence from the American States." *Review of Economics and Statistics* 88 (1, February): 182–86.

Feng, Juan, Taye Mengistae, and Yutaka Yoshino. 2009. "Foreign Premium on Productivity among Enterprises in Africa." Analytical background note prepared for the study.

Greif, Avner. 1993. "Contract Enforceability and Economic Institutions in Early Trade: The Maghribi Traders' Coalition." *American Economic Review* 83 (3): 525–48.

Gunning, Jan Willem, and Taye Mengistae. 2001. "Determinants of African Manufacturing Investment: The Microeconomic Evidence." *Journal of African Economies* 10 (supplement 2): 48–80.

Hewitt Associates. 2006. Improving Business Competitiveness and Increasing Economic Growth in Ghana: The Role of Information and Communications Technologies.

Honohan, Patrick, and Thorsten Beck. 2007. *Making Finance Work for Africa.* Washington, DC: World Bank.

Jann, Ben. 2008. "The Blinder-Oaxaca Decomposition for Linear Regression Model." *Stata Journal* 88 (4): 453–79.

Mengistae, Taye, and Catherine A. Pattillo. 2004. "Export Orientation and Productivity in Sub-Saharan Africa." *IMF Staff Papers* 51 (2): 327–53.

Milner, Chris, and Verena Tandrayen. 2004. "The Impact of Exporting and Export Destination on Manufacturing Wages: Evidence for Sub-Saharan Africa." CREDIT Research Paper 04/01, University of Nottingham, Nottingham, U.K.

O'Donnell, Owen, Eddy van Doorslaer, Adam Wagstaff, and Magnus Lindelow. 2008. "Analyzing Health Equity Using Household Survey Data." World Bank, Washington, DC. www.worldbank.org/analyzinghealthequit.

Ramachandran, Vijaya, Alan Gelb, and Manju Shah. 2009. *Africa's Private Sector: What's Wrong with the Business Environment and What to Do about It.* Washington, DC: Center for Global Development.

Rankin, Neil, Måns Söderbom, and Francis Teal. 2006. "Exporting from manufacturing firms in Sub-Saharan Africa." *Journal of African Economies* 15(4): 671–87.

Rauch, James. 2001a. "Black Ties Only? Ethnic Business Networks, Intermediaries, and African American Retail Entrepreneurship." In *Networks and Markets,* ed. James Rauch and Alessandra Casella, 270–309. New York: Russell Sage Foundation.

———. 2001b. "Business and Social Networks in International Trade." *Journal of Economic Literature* 39 (4): 1177–203.

Rauch, James, and Vitor Trindade. 2002. "Ethnic Chinese Networks in International Trade." *Review of Economics and Statistics* 84 (1): 116–30.

Roberts, Mark J., and James R. Tybout. 1997. "The Decision to Export in Colombia: An Empirical Model of Entry with Sunk Costs." *American Economic Review* 87 (4): 545–64.

Soderböm, Måns, and Francis Teal. 2002. "Are Manufacturing Exports the Key to Economic Success in Africa?" Unpublished mss., University of Oxford, Oxford, U.K.

Yoshino, Yutaka. 2008. "Domestic Constraints, Firm Characteristics, and Geographical Diversification of Firm-Level Manufacturing Exports in Africa." Policy Research Working Paper 4574, World Bank, Washington, DC.

CHAPTER 3

Industrial Clusters as Natural Agglomerations of Micro and Small Enterprises: A Conceptual Framework

Chapter 2 identifies capital intensity, manager's educational background, and access to nonlocal markets as major factors contributing to the foreign-domestic gap in business performance in Africa. Removing the constraints facing domestic enterprises in those areas would improve their business performance and ability to catch up with foreign-owned enterprises operating in Africa. Productivity is the key factor facilitating market access for domestic enterprises, but firm size explains a large part of the performance gap between domestic and foreign enterprises. The vast majority of domestic enterprises in Africa are micro and small in size, and size is clearly the most significant binding constraint for domestic enterprises.

One obvious approach to determining how firm size constrains the growth of micro and small enterprises is to examine the factors that facilitate their growth. Some studies have found that human capital and the manager's level of education affect the size and growth of firms (for example, McPherson 1996; Ramachandran and Shah 1999; Ramachandran, Gelb, and Shah 2009; Mengistae 2006; Akoten and Otsuka 2007). Others have looked at investment behavior as the most straightforward way for enterprises to grow in size. Research based on data from the Regional Program on Enterprise Development finds that micro and small enterprises in Africa are not investing as much as expected. Constraints on access to finance limit the scope for firms' new investment. Another reason could be that high transaction costs and high risks in doing business hamper the incentives to invest. For example, in a study on firm-level data from Cameroon, Ghana, Kenya, and Zimbabwe on the lack of firm investment (Gunning and Mengistae (2001) find that large risks, rather than access to finance, are what matter. The cost of physical capital is also high in Africa. Artadi and Sala-i-Martin (2004) note that investment in African countries yields considerably less expansion of productive capacity because the prices of capital goods in Sub-Saharan Africa relative to the prices of consumption goods are 70 percent higher than in high-income countries and countries in East Asia.

Another approach to the question of how size constrains growth is to analyze coping mechanisms, such as physical agglomeration, that micro and small enterprises use to overcome their size constraint. In order to survive, micro and small enterprises find ways to get around the size constraint. The functions, efficiency, and constraints of these coping mechanisms need to be better understood if public policies are to be formulated to integrate those enterprises with the formal economy.

Physical agglomeration is one of these mitigating mechanisms for micro and small enterprises. Groups of micro and small enterprises undertaking similar industrial activities in specific locations are common in major African cities. These enterprises are often informal, are housed in simple structures, and use simple technologies. In many cases, the term "workshop" characterizes their workspace better than the term "factory." This type of *industrial cluster* is common across Africa.

Clusters provide a wide range of benefits to participating enterprises across different stages of their development. Clustering facilitates explicit and implicit economic benefits for participating enterprises. The trust and peer pressure that naturally develop within clusters provide the basis for joint actions to invest in common facilities and infrastructure and facilitate smoother commercial transactions, reducing transaction costs and risks. Clusters offer enterprises opportunities for consolidated market access and offer consumers greater choice as well as convenience by reducing search costs. Implicit knowledge spillovers among enterprises are significant externalities, reducing the fixed costs of investing in research and development. New entrants to clusters start by imitating what incumbents do in the clusters. As shown in subsequent chapters, those features are observed at various stages of cluster development within Africa, including informal survival-level clusters as well as nontraditional, more dynamic clusters such as agro-processing, tourism, and information technology (IT) clusters.

This chapter presents a theoretical framework for discussing the role that these geographic agglomerations of industrial activities—industrial clusters—play in enhancing business performance and market participation for micro and small enterprises and determining the constraints that exist inside clusters. Although started as horizontal associations of the same industries, some spontaneously formed industrial clusters in Africa have succeeded in expanding the scope of their activities by attracting related industries and services through backward and forward linkages, thus developing vertical value chains.

This study focuses on spontaneously grown natural industrial clusters, mostly in light manufacturing, rather than policy-based constructed zones or policy-driven cluster development initiatives that are not necessarily based on geographic concentrations. There are two main types of industrial agglomerations around the world. One type is created deliberately by government policies, such as the establishment of industrial parks, to attract certain industries, including foreign investors, to specific locations. The other forms and grows spontaneously by the natural agglomeration force of private industries based on their commercial incentives. This report focuses on the latter type of industrial agglomeration. Many clusters fall in between spontaneously formed natural clusters and policy-driven artificial clusters, and it is not easy to distinguish one clearly from the other. Our empirical focus is on spontaneously grown natural clusters that have received only limited government support.

The mechanism through which agglomeration occurs has often been discussed in the economic geography literature. As explained later in this chapter, agglomeration can result in positive effects when firms agglomerate in certain locations due to technical spillovers, labor market pooling, and availability of specialized inputs and services and thus form backward and forward linkages. These externalities are often called Marshallian externalities, because they were first introduced in Alfred Marshall's seminal work *Principles of Economics* (Marshall 1920). Firms perceive these externalities as resulting in profitability, and profitability attracts even more firms.

In addition to these agglomeration externalities, industrial clusters could be a mechanism for micro and small enterprises in Africa to counter the weak general business environment in which transaction costs and risks are high. The proximity of other firms reduces the transaction costs for individual firms, which would otherwise be high as a result of inherent market failures, such as incomplete contracts or asymmetric information as well as insufficient formal market institutions to correct such market failures. Government failures, such as excessively strict licensing and regulatory regimes, also contribute to high transaction costs for doing business. One clear example of how clustering helps enterprises to get around high transaction costs is that clusters reduce the search costs of identifying buyers and suppliers. The strong knowledge-sharing environment of clusters fosters trust relationships among cluster-based entrepreneurs, since deviations from community norms in business conduct are discouraged by the reputational risks that entrepreneurs face in such an environment.

The following section describes the concept of industrial clusters and places it in a theoretical framework to identify a set of analytical issues addressed in later chapters.

Concept of Clusters

An industrial cluster is an agglomeration of specific industrial activities and related services in a geographically small area. This concept captures both spatial and sectoral aspects. There is no specific agreement in the literature as to how narrowly or broadly spatial and sectoral units should be set to define industrial clusters. However, whether or not a particular concentration of industries is recognized as an "industrial cluster" may well depend on whether agglomeration dynamics exist that improve the productivity of firms within such a concentration.

Industrial clusters can be conceptually framed either ex post for analytical purposes or ex ante for developmental purposes. For example, industrial clusters and industrial parks are different concepts, but they could overlap in real examples. Some industrial parks could be considered industrial clusters ex post if they have key features of clustering (spatial and sectoral concentration and agglomeration dynamics). However, programs to develop industrial clusters should be differentiated from those to develop industrial parks.[1]

The various types of industrial clusters are described in box 3.1. This study focuses on industrial clusters that have been formed spontaneously and populated by micro and small enterprises. The vast majority of those enterprises are in the informal sector. These clusters are what Altenburg and Meyer-Stamer (1999) call a "survival cluster of micro and small-scale enterprises" that produce generally low-quality products and sell them

Box 3.1

Typology of Industrial Clusters

Industrial clusters are formed in three ways (see table B3.1). Some are "constructed" by deliberate government efforts to support development of domestic industries or to attract foreign investment in the economy. Such constructed clusters may be formed as export-processing zones (EPZs) and industrial parks. Industrial parks and EPZs, while not necessarily the same as industrial clusters, can be considered industrial clusters if they attract businesses and related goods and services in specific sectors. In some cases, such as the Gerezani metalwork cluster in Dar es Salaam, Tanzania, clusters were formed by deliberate government action to empower local production by micro, small, and medium enterprises. However, most clusters in developing countries are spontaneous agglomerations of enterprises. Sometimes agglomeration occurs as a by-product of policy changes (for example, Suame Magazine in Kumasi, Ghana), as a local response to large foreign investments, or as a result of exogenously introduced triggers, most notably new foreign direct investment (FDI); for example, the Tianjin cluster in China developed around a new Toyota plant.

Table B3.1   Examples of Clusters in Africa

Dimension and type	Examples
Origin	
Constructed zones	Textile and garment EPZ (Mauritius), Hsinchu Science Park (Taiwan, China), Casablanca Techno Park (Morocco), industrial parks (Vietnam), automobile industry (China)
Spontaneous	Suame Magazine (Kumasi, Ghana), Nairobi cut-flower cluster (Kenya), Otigba computer cluster (Nigeria), Sinos Valley shoe cluster (Brazil), Sialkot surgical instrument cluster (Pakistan)
Exogenous trigger (for example, FDI)	Bangalore IT cluster (India), Tianjin cluster (China)
Institutional support	
Government driven	Guangzhou automobile industry cluster (China)
Private sector driven	Bangalore IT cluster (India)
Mix (public-private partnership)	Numerous examples
Spatial concentration	
Confined and tightly concentrated (geographically intact)	*Jua Kali* manufacturing clusters (Kenya)

(continued next page)

Box 3.1 *(continued)*

Table B3.1   Examples of Clusters in Africa

Dimension and type	Examples
Not confined (relatively wide geographic spread)	Textile and garment EPZ (Mauritius), Western Cape wine cluster (South Africa)
Geographic spread	
Provincial (multiple municipalities)	Western Cape wine cluster (South Africa)
Municipality	Arusha furniture cluster (Tanzania)
District (within a municipality)	Suame Magazine (Ghana), *Jua Kali* (Kenya)
Market	
Local	Numerous examples
Export (regional)	Suame Magazine (Kumasi, Ghana), Uhuru Market (Nairobi, Kenya)
Export (global, developed countries)	Lake Victoria fishing cluster (Kenya), Nairobi cut-flower cluster (Kenya), Sinos Valley shoe cluster (Brazil), Sialkot surgical instrument cluster (Pakistan)

Source: Yoshino 2009.

Industrial clusters can also be categorized by the type of institutional support received. Industrial clusters often receive external and internal institutional support, which can come from the government, the private sector, or both. For example, Texas Instruments played a key role in setting up infrastructure (a satellite cable system) in the IT cluster in Bangalore, India, and government efforts followed the take-off of the sector (Pack and Saggi 2006). In some cases, clusters receive support based on a public-private partnership between government and local private sector associations.

Some clusters contain enterprises within confined areas or zones. Enterprises in such clusters have plants and offices within marked or unmarked boundaries and are essentially contiguous. In other clusters, enterprises coexist with other establishments (for example, residential buildings) in mixed land use areas and are not necessarily contiguous. Some clusters have loosely defined boundaries, but are still geographically intact. Many spatially confined clusters are defined by government intervention, for example, by establishing zoning policies as well as providing at least some public support for infrastructure (for example, government-provided simple factory roofs in Kenya's *Jua Kali*). However, in some clusters, which usually cover wider geographic areas, participating enterprises are more widely distributed. The type of industry or sector often influences the geographic scale of clusters. For example, clusters of agro-processing products tend to cover larger geographic areas due to their linkage with land-based agriculture (for example, the Western Cape wine cluster in South Africa).

Related to spatial integrity and contiguity, the geographic scale of clusters varies from the level of province, city, town, and village to inner-city district, neighborhood, and street. For the larger geographic scale, cluster-based firms are not confined to an exclusive area, but are spread across the province or the city.

While the majority of clusters in developing countries produce products sold only in local or national markets, some produce products for export to regional and global markets. In some cases, such as Suame Magazine in Kumasi, Ghana, consumers of services provided by the cluster come not only from elsewhere in Ghana but also from neighboring countries such as Burkina Faso and even Nigeria.

Source: Yoshino 2009.

predominantly to domestic markets. This type of spontaneous survival cluster is quite prevalent in Sub-Saharan Africa.

Economic Geography of Industrial Clusters

Enterprises are attracted to industrial agglomerations because profitability is higher inside them. Agglomeration leads to improved productivity—hence higher profitability—that results from the following three types of positive Marshallian externalities (Marshall 1920):

- *Technological spillover.* Geographic proximity among enterprises facilitates formal and informal interactions through which industry-specific and location-specific knowledge and skills are shared among enterprises in either explicit or tacit ways. Such diffusion of industrial knowledge may take place horizontally between producers or vertically between producers and input suppliers, traders, and other service providers.
- *Labor market pooling.* A concentration of enterprises engaged in the same or similar industries creates a pool of labor with skills specific to those industries. Such pooling attracts additional labor with relevant skills from outside. A typical example is the availability of

human resources in the film and entertainment industries in Holly-
wood, California.

- *Specialized intermediate inputs and services.* Agglomeration of industries
also attracts specialized suppliers of inputs and services. Similar to the
labor market pooling effect, specialized suppliers of inputs and services
emerge both internally (for example, some cluster-based enterpreneurs
shifting from producers to providers of business support services) and
externally (attracting outside suppliers and services).

The economic geography model (more precisely "new economic geography" model) provides a framework for understanding how economic
activities can concentrate in certain areas.[2] The model asserts that transportation costs can lead industries to agglomerate in certain locations to
capture the agglomeration externalities discussed above.[3] With prohibi-
tively high transportation costs, a priori, industries are dispersed across various locations, because it is optimal for firms to be located close to
consumers. The extreme opposite occurs when there are no transportation
costs. With no transportation costs, industries are again dispersed across
various locations because location per se does not create any productivity
differential. With an intermediate level of transportation costs, co-location
with local consumers brings smaller benefits to firms than co-location with
other firms because of agglomeration externalities among firms. This is
particularly true when product differentiation (and division of tasks)
encourages firms to build interfirm networks of intermediate input suppliers and buyers. These interfirm linkages, as well as transportation cost savings in firm-to-firm shipping of materials, lead to physical agglomeration
of industries in specific locations.

Essentially, the positive externalities drive agglomeration. Product differentiation enables firms to build buyer-supplier relationships of intermediate inputs (both goods and services) locally within clusters. This
makes co-locating with other firms producing differentiated products
attractive. A skilled labor force that moves into locations where industries agglomerate also enhances the benefits of co-locating with other
firms. The increased supply of skilled labor and providers of intermediate
inputs (both goods and services) generates gains in efficiency and productivity among producers of final goods in the cluster (*backward linkage
effect*). The higher productivity attracts more firms to the cluster, which
creates new demand for skilled labor and specialized intermediate inputs
of both goods and services (*forward linkage effect*). The backward and forward linkage effects within clusters are illustrated in figure 3.1.[4]

Figure 3.1   Backward and Forward Linkages and Agglomeration

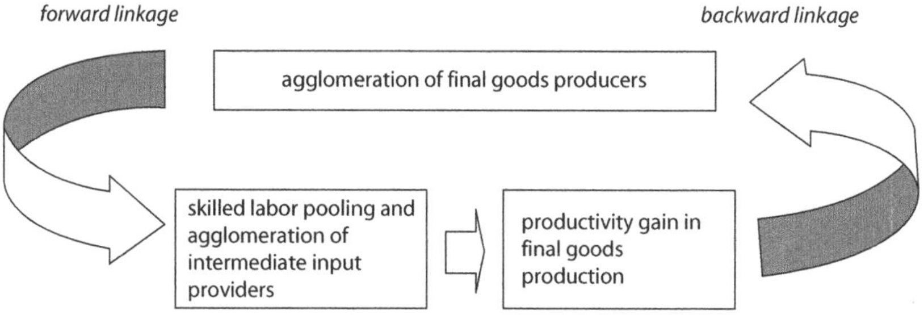

forward linkage   *backward linkage*

agglomeration of final goods producers

skilled labor pooling and agglomeration of intermediate input providers

productivity gain in final goods production

Source: Yoshino 2009.

According to the economic geography model, the pattern of dispersion and agglomeration of industries in geographic space rests on the balance between agglomeration forces (more technically, *centripetal forces*) and dispersion forces (*centrifugal forces*). Agglomeration forces attract firms to locate close to one another, while dispersion forces make firms locate apart from one another. The most typical dispersion force comes from negative externalities resulting from congestion. Concentration of economic activities may also reduce productivity by crowding out physical space (literally creating congestion) as well as market space (increasing wages and the price of land), resulting in lower profitability for the agglomerated firms. Those negative implications of physical concentrations are collectively called congestion effects.

Beyond Transportation Costs: Market and Government Failures, Transaction Costs, and Industrial Clusters

In the context of development, the economic geography framework of industrial agglomeration needs to be augmented with other factors, the most important being transaction costs generated by market failures and government failures. Transaction costs are high in developing economies in Africa, as well as in other regions, because of inherent market failures from incomplete contracts, information asymmetry, and lack of proper market institutions to mitigate such market failures. Government failures, such as inefficient and burdensome regulations, also contribute to the high transaction costs of doing business in Africa. In an environment of high transaction costs, informal social networks, such as ethnic networks, can reduce transaction costs, including search costs, and facilitate information flows based on a trust relationship among members.[5] Ethnic networks help entrepreneurs within an ethnic group to obtain finance and build buyer-supplier relationships with other members of the group.

Another type of informal network is based on a trust relationship developed in location-based communities, which is another reason why firms, particularly micro and small firms, agglomerate in developing countries. Sonobe and Otsuka (2006a) argue that industrial clusters facilitate market transactions by reducing transaction costs. Owing to the enterprises' geographic proximity, information about the technological capacities of individual enterprises, their marketing behavior, and the conduct and personality of their managers is public knowledge within the cluster. At a micro level, ethnicity plays a specific role in cluster formation as well. Data from the Japan International Cooperation Agency study of a furniture cluster in Arusha, Tanzania, presented in chapter 5, show that owners of furniture workshops choose to locate in a subcluster of workshops owned by people from the same ethnic group.

The strong knowledge-sharing environment of clusters fosters trust relationships among cluster-based entrepreneurs because deviations from community norms in business conduct are discouraged by the reputational risks that entrepreneurs face in such an environment. If an owner's reputation is questionable, the enterprise will lose customers and may eventually face bankruptcy. Morosini (2004) characterizes industrial clusters as "social communities." Small-scale entrepreneurs form clusters as a mechanism for coping with high transaction costs that are associated with information asymmetry and incomplete contracts in the general market environment.

Clusters also provide a mechanism for correcting coordination failures among firms by avoiding the "hold-up" problem in making investments that benefit multiple firms through buyer-supplier relationships. In the literature on industrial clusters, this "correction" is related to the concept of "collective efficiency," which Schmitz and Nadvi (1999) define as the "competitive advantage derived from external economies and joint action" in industrial clusters. In their concept of collective efficiency, positive agglomeration externalities represent "passive" collective efficiency, while joint action represents "active" efficiency. Joint action is the notion that firms may consciously choose to cooperate and collaborate. Schmitz and Nadvi argue that clusters emerge and their growth depends on whether participating firms have agreed to cooperate with each other in providing intra-cluster public goods (for example, sharing infrastructure such as storage or training facilities), coordinating their actions, and internalizing agglomeration externalities. Joint actions can also alleviate negative conges-tion effects (for example, pollution controls). In a few examples of indus-trial clusters, such joint actions are brokered through cluster associations and leadership by senior entrepreneurs who have been operating in the clusters longer than others. In some cases leading enterprises in the clusters voluntarily provide public goods that are not related directly to commercial transactions, such as meeting space for cluster associations, which facilitate the exchange of knowledge among cluster-based entrepreneurs.

External Linkages and Cluster Competitiveness

The standard economic geography model described earlier provides a good framework for understanding the clustering of industries from a global (general equilibrium) point of view. The three key features of the frame-work are (1) endogenous agglomeration forces and balance between agglomeration and dispersion forces, (2) the self-reinforcing mechanism of agglomeration through backward and forward linkages with clusters, and (3) market access beyond the cluster or the local market through reduced friction in trading or, more specifically, reduced transportation and transac-tion costs. The spatial economics framework of industrial clusters is, in fact, quite similar to the "diamond model" of competitive advantage developed by Michael Porter (see figure 3.2).

One of the most significant implications of this framework of indus-trial clusters from a spatial economic point of view is that the external market linkages of cluster-based firms are as important as intra-cluster networks of firms (that is, market access beyond the cluster or the local market). Although localized agglomeration externalities, in conjunction with savings from transportation and transaction costs within a location, support initial cluster formation, a cluster will not grow unless member firms have good linkages with external markets (consumers), other firms inside and outside the cluster (input providers), and factors of production (skilled labor and technology).

Agglomeration forces produce a strong lock-in effect, retaining firms already in the cluster and attracting others from outside. This lock-in effect works positively to encourage the growth of clusters in their initial stage, but becomes negative in the long run by deterring innovation and sustained growth. Internal systems and culture become less flexible in adopting new ideas and systems as agglomeration continues. Because of the self-reinforcing mechanism of agglomeration through backward and forward linkage effects, clusters can lock in suboptimal levels of skills

Figure 3.2   Porter's Diamond Model

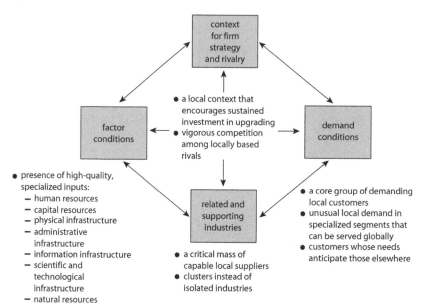

Source: Porter 1985.

and technology in the absence of mechanisms to upgrade from within the cluster. Suppose a cluster is surrounded by a labor market in which the skill level is lower than elsewhere in the economy. Then the labor market pooling effect would cause firms in the cluster to be locked into inferior skills and technology. Thus the cluster's external linkages— which are formed by maintaining access to nonlocal markets for sales, inputs, capital, skilled labor, and technology—are essential to avoid such rigidity in the internal system and overcome the negative lock-in effect from clustering (Fujita 2003).

Internal Dynamics and External Linkages in Industrial Clusters around the World

There are several ways to analyze the performance of clusters. Some scholars assess the internal dynamics of individual industrial clusters around the world. Some ask how agglomeration externalities and joint action, the basic components of the collective efficiency framework developed by Schmitz and Nadvi (1999), are working in the chosen clusters. Still others look at clusters' external linkages, such as linkages with foreign investment and export markets. The vast majority of studies provide basic quantitative information to describe the size and the growth of specific industrial clusters, but only provide qualitative anecdotal evidence to support their arguments for how cluster dynamics work within these clusters.[6]

The characteristics of clusters vary substantially with regard to the development context in which they exist. Schmitz and Nadvi (1999) consider two development stages of industrial clusters: "incipient" clusters and "mature" clusters. Incipient clusters in the early stage of industrial development with regard to firms' products, technologies, and skills are found mostly in low-income economies.[7] The notion of "survival" clusters described by Altenburg and Meyer-Stamer (1999) is similar to that of incipient clusters. In contrast, firms in mature clusters produce relatively advanced products using higher technologies and skills and operate in global markets, either through export markets or through linkages with major foreign investments.[8] The distinction between incipient and mature clusters is somewhat blurry. For example, some clusters that could be classified as incipient because they operate with low-level technologies nonetheless export globally to industrial countries and subsequently face technical barriers in such markets (for example, Lake Victoria fishing clusters).

The characteristics of industrial clusters around the world are highly heterogeneous. Comparing their performance quantitatively with the same yardstick is not feasible. In this chapter, we maintain a general format for summarizing findings on the performance of clusters, with regard to both their internal dynamics and their external linkages.

Case studies on industrial clusters provide solid evidence of agglomeration externalities in individual clusters. Although not necessarily measured scientifically, the strength of the externalities and the magnitude of efficiency gains from clusters vary substantially across cases. Generally speaking, in clusters where joint actions among firms take place, the agglomeration effects seem to be positive.

Labor Pooling

The labor pooling effect can be observed in almost any cluster. For example, the Sialkot surgical instrument cluster in Pakistan, the Gamarra garment cluster in Lima, Peru, the Agra footwear cluster in India, and the Suame Magazine cluster in Kumasi, Ghana, are all supported by large pools of workers with specialized skills and a flexible, functioning labor market. In measuring the performance gap between clustered and dispersed small and medium enterprises in Lima, Visser (1999) observes that clustered producers in Gamarra depend less on family labor than firms outside the cluster, and if they do depend on family members, the relatives receive payment. Not only were those clusters built on existing concentrations of skilled labor, but they also attract migrant workers from elsewhere.

Upgrading the level of skills within a cluster is very important. McCormick (1999) observes that some clusters in Sub-Saharan Africa experience a labor "disabling" effect, where the new pool of labor being attracted to the cluster does not possess sufficient skills ex ante, with the result that the agglomeration of labor does not upgrade the cluster.[9] Agglomeration force attracts not only workers with specialized skills, but also workers without such skills if there is an insufficient supply of the former. Skill upgrading within a cluster is important not only for avoiding this type of disabling effect but also for supporting the cluster's growth and survival (from external competition). Like other African clusters populated by micro enterprises, the vast majority of workers in the cluster of Suame Magazine do not have postsecondary education and are employed through informal family connections. Zeng (2008) notes that the cluster is facing an oversupply of new entrants as a result of low entry barriers and low level technology. Similarly, the lack of skills among workers in the Lake Victoria fishing clusters (in Uganda as well as Kenya) has been a critical bottleneck for upgrading the technological level of cluster operations (Oyelaran-Oyeyinka and McCormick 2007).

Many studies show that the existence of a sufficient pool of skilled labor at the local level is a precondition for a cluster's success. The success of IT clusters such as the one in Bangalore is critically dependent on the local pool of educated workers (Kuchiki and Tsuji 2005). This requirement applies to FDI-driven clusters such as those in Vietnam, because foreign investors' choice of location is significantly influenced by the local availability of skilled workers at relatively low cost. Similarly, a preexisting skilled labor market is an important condition for export-oriented clusters such as in Sialkot, Pakistan.

Knowledge Spillover and Innovation

The very nature of industrial clusters—physical proximity and common (or similar) industrial activities among firms—makes knowledge and technological spillovers among firms relatively easy. In the Ludhiana woolen knitwear cluster in India, Tewari (1999) documents how market-specific knowledge held among a group of exporters to Western Europe has diffused to other firms in the cluster, helping the cluster to improve its export competitiveness after economic liberalization in 1991. The Otigba computer cluster in Nigeria has been successful in expanding the core technology of firms through apprenticeships and knowledge sharing.

In many clusters in developing countries, external knowledge and technologies play an important role in providing the initial step toward innovation. The most illustrative external source is FDI, as seen in many clusters in East Asia, such as industrial clusters in China and Vietnam.

In some cases, internal sources play a more significant role in innovation. For example, in the Ludhiana metalworking cluster, firms' cost-cutting improvements and low-cost adaptation and replication of machinery allowed small firms to upgrade their production processes at a relatively rapid rate and low cost. As with the labor force, the pre-existing quality of firms' knowledge could be an important factor in determining whether innovation truly works within a cluster. In other words, what an entrepreneur already knows is important (Oyelaran-Oyeyinka and McCormick 2007).

How can firms upgrade skills within a cluster? In some clusters, particularly those in high-tech industries such as the IT cluster in Bangalore, firms train their employees to be competitive within the cluster (Kuchiki and Tsuji 2005). Many clusters have training facilities and programs that are public goods provided by local manufacturing associations or cooperatives, an example of the "joint action" notion of Schmitz and Nadvi (1999). Many such training facilities and programs receive financial support from international donors, including bilateral and multilateral development agencies and nongovernmental organizations. Whether such institutions lead to technological upgrading varies among clusters. The case studies of African industrial clusters compiled by Oyelaran-Oyeyinka and McCormick (2007) suggest that training institutions do not make much effort to offer programs relevant to the businesses in nearby clusters.[10]

Regardless of whether knowledge and technologies are acquired externally or internally, the mechanism of innovation is critical for cluster growth. Akoten, Otsuka, and Sonobe (2006), in the context of a shoe cluster in Addis Ababa, Ethiopia, observe that the cluster's growth has been driven not only by the entry of new enterprises, but also by the growth of innovative enterprises and followers; moreover, highly educated entrepreneurs introduce new ideas on product design, production methods, production and labor management, procurement, and marketing, because they face fierce competition from a swarm of micro enterprises that are highly efficient producers of standard products.

Based on a series of empirical studies of specific industrial clusters in Asia (China, India, Japan, and Taiwan, China) as well as in Africa (Ethiopia, Ghana, and Kenya), Sonobe and Otsuka (2006b) summarize what they call an "endogenous model" of industrial development through industrial clusters (see table 3.1).

Interfirm Linkages and Market Access

Backward and forward linkages are generally visible in the vast majority of clusters. Zeng (2008) documents the cases of different clusters in Africa (for example, Lake Victoria fishing, Otigba computer village, Suame Magazine) in forming cluster-based value chains in which firms share mass clientele, synergies, knowledge networks, and infrastructure (including facilities and services). In fact, clusters provide a mechanism for correcting coordination failures among firms by facilitating necessary investments that benefit multiple firms at the same time. Cluster-based enterprises that have developed a trust relationship can take joint action by choosing to cooperate and collaborate on investing in public goods (for example, sharing infrastructure such as storage or training facilities) and mitigating common problems such as pollution (see box 3.2). Clusters around the world owe their success to strong joint action among participating entrepreneurs.

Table 3.1   An Endogenous Model of Industrial Development

Phase	Prior experience of managers	Education	Innovation, imitation, productivity growth	Institution
Initiation	Merchants and engineers	Low	Imitated foreign technology directly or indirectly	Internal production of parts, components, and final products
Quantity expansion	Spinoffs and entry from various fields	Mixed	Imitated technology, stagnant productivity, and declining profitability	Market transactions, division of labor, and formation of industrial cluster
Quality improvement	Second generation of founders and newcomers with new ideas	Very high	Multifaceted innovations, exit of many enterprises, and increasing productivity	Reputation and brand names, direct sales, subcontracts or vertical integration, and emergence of large enterprises

Source: Sonobe and Otsuka 2006b.

Box 3.2

Clusters and the Environment

The spatial concentration of industrial clusters has negative environmental externalities, such as local pollution. In large-scale industrial clusters in Asian countries, pollution in industrial clusters is a serious and growing concern for policy makers. In India the Central Pollution and Control Board in consultation with the Ministry of Environment and Forest recently conducted a study to assess the level of pollution among 43 industrial clusters in the country, applying the comprehensive environmental pollution index. Pollution is also a problem in industrial clusters in Africa. A furniture cluster in Kumasi, Ghana, has received a growing number of complaints of water pollution in the neighboring areas. Joint action within clusters to address the problem is increasingly important, and proper public policy interventions may be necessary.

At the same time, industrial clusters could take innovative approaches to addressing environmental problems by leveraging joint actions among enterprises. For example, industrial waste generated within clusters could be used to create new opportunities for businesses, as observed in the development of industries using scrap metals in Suame Magazine (Aryeetey, Owusu, and Quartey 2009). Firms could also save costs by collaborating on waste disposal and recycling. Some clusters have taken collective action to modernize equipment (such as testing tools) to comply with sanitary and phytosanitary standards in the European Union market, as in the fish-processing cluster in Kisumu, Kenya, for their exports of Nile perch from Lake Victoria.

Source: Authors.

Interfirm linkages through buyer-supplier relations and subcontracting, which are the core factor in thickening backward and forward linkages as well as facilitating knowledge spillovers within clusters, are also visible in some clusters in Sub-Saharan Africa as well as elsewhere. Subcontracting is the most visible form of "joint action" among firms within clusters. For example, subcontracting is prevalent in Suame Magazine in Ghana, in cut-flower clusters in Kenya, and in handicrafts clusters in Mwenge and furniture clusters in Keko, both in Tanzania, according to Zeng (2008).

The extent to which operational networks are developed within a cluster depends on the degree of specialization of tasks within it. In

India's Ludhiana cluster, firms try to economize their operations by developing an extensive system of local subcontracting and task-based specializations that help to lower costs and spread risks. This extensive division of labor attracts upstream and downstream industries to the region, such as finishing services, distribution providers, and capital goods producers, which over time have deepened the region's industrial structure (Tewari 1999).

Clusters in more mature stages produce technologically more advanced products than clusters in incipient stages, and their products are often exported to international markets, where they face global competitors. Those clusters are affected directly by developments in trade policies, such as import liberalization and increased competition with imported products. Competitiveness in export markets is crucial for those clusters with regard to both price and quality. While producing technologically more advanced products or higher-quality products allows firms in clusters to expand their market access to nonlocal markets, including export markets, some aspects of industrial organization related to backward and forward linkages play a pivotal role in facilitating market expansion.

As noted by Sonobe and Otsuka (2006a) for Asian clusters or by Oyelaran-Oyeyinka and McCormick (2007) for African clusters, trader-manufacturer networks play a pivotal role in linking cluster-based products and nonlocal markets. Sonobe and Otsuka (2006a) note that some cluster-based innovation is driven by merchants (as opposed to producers or engineers). A trader network is particularly effective when cluster-based producers are located in specifically confined or zoned areas (Akoten and Otsuka 2007). Using survey data of local micro and small garment producers in several clusters in Nairobi, Akoten and Otsuka (2007) show that well-educated and highly socially networked tailors who are capable of producing a certain quality of product are likely to link up with traders to become micro manufacturers over time, suggesting that transactions with traders enable micro manufacturers to outperform tailors, helping to transform the mode of industrial production in developing economies.

Unlike clusters in the early stage of industrialization, more mature clusters—the Sialkot surgical instrument cluster in Pakistan, Sinos shoe cluster in Brazil, and the shoe cluster in Guadalajara, Mexico—tend to be forced to perform to global standards in matters not just of costs, but also of quality, including timely responses to new developments in market access (in particular, nontariff barriers) in export markets. In these clusters, effective joint actions, horizontal actions among cluster-based firms, as well as vertical actions between cluster-based firms and intermediaries and buyers in export markets have been an important factor in facilitating and sustaining their market access in the event of changes in market conditions abroad. In the case of export-oriented clusters such as Sialkot, firms acquire important knowledge from foreign buyers of their products. In the Sialkot cluster, German firms sent metallurgical engineers to train the Sialkot partner firm in quality control and production engineering (Nadvi 1996, 1999).[11] In Guadalajara, trade liberalization (for example, Mexico's accession to the General Agreement on Tariffs and Trade in the late 1980s) improved both horizontal and vertical cooperation among cluster-based firms in information exchange, technological assistance, quality control, negotiation on payment and delivery conditions, and setting of product specifications.

Some clusters in East Asia were carefully located in areas that could simultaneously pursue enhanced interfirm linkages and new advantages in market access. The development of Eastern Seaboard in Thailand, which started with a massive infrastructure investment to attract export-oriented FDI, was accompanied by an extensive effort linking FDI firms with domestic suppliers ("reverse trade fair" by the Japan External Trade Organization). As a result, Eastern Seaboard has become the hub of an automobile value chain network in East Asia involving a wide variety of domestic suppliers effectively linked to the export market. Similar mechanisms are observed in Dalian, China, and northern Vietnam (Muto, Takeuchi, and Koike 2007).

Role of Clusters in Micro and Small Enterprise Development

The conceptual framework of industrial clusters and the summary of empirical evidence presented above highlight the following hypotheses on the role of industrial clusters in helping micro and small enterprises to overcome their size constraints and enhance their business performance in Africa.

- *Cluster-level economies of scale.* As a mechanism to overcome size constraints, there could be cluster-level economies of scale in enhancing firm-level business performance as opposed to firm-level economies of scale. What are the potential roles of networks among manufacturers (for example, subcontracting) inside and outside of clusters?

- *External market linkage.* The conceptual framework has made a clear case that external linkages with nonlocal markets and actors (suppliers, buyers, and consumers) are critical for clusters to grow and avoid negative lock-in effects, as discussed in Fujita (2003). In many cases, access to external markets and access to technologies are key factors in the growth of industrial clusters. This applies to the question not only of whether firms can export or not, but also whether they can expand market space from the local to the national level and form links to foreign investments.
- *Networks.* Clusters provide a basis for building strong horizontal networks. But more specifically, what are the roles of cluster-based interfirm "joint actions" to overcome information asymmetry and build trust relationships among firms? How do business associations work?

At the same time, industrial clusters of micro and small enterprises may face the following new issues:

- *Competition and congestion.* The agglomeration forces continue to attract new entrants to clusters, which increases competition within the clusters and reduces profitability for incumbents. The physical concentration of enterprises also raises the costs of space (high rent, physical congestion).
- *Skills and innovation.* As in the case of a "disabling labor effect," as discussed in Oyelaran-Oyeyinka and McCormick (2007), what often matters is the surrounding investment climate, including the availability of factors necessary for production (skilled labor, access to finance). Do cluster-based enterprises have sufficient factors of production? What about the quality of such factors?
- *Growth and transformation.* How do cluster-based enterprises grow and even transform to become larger enterprises? How do firms move from "survival" clusters to formal industrial areas? Which factors facilitate their mobility?
- *Competition among clusters under new spatial developments.* As predicted by the economic geography model, with an intermediate level of transportation costs, co-location with other firms is beneficial. Africa is witnessing a series of regional connectivity projects that are changing the level of transportation costs and widening the scope of the market in which firms and consumers search for each other. In such a context, can a cluster maintain an advantage over other clusters that have joined the same market sphere? Is there a case for formulating larger agglomerations?

Notes

1. World Bank (2009) has a useful summary of how industrial clusters differ from industrial parks, EPZs, and industrial policies.

2. The new economic geography model (including its variants) is a general-equilibrium model that explains agglomeration of industries and labor force. The core-periphery model, developed by Paul Krugman (1991), has key features of the so-called "new trade theory" based on the Dixit-Stiglitz framework (Dixit and Stiglitz 1977). These include increasing returns to scale, monopolistic competition on differentiated products, and constant elasticity of substitution demand. The model is often applied to address economic questions in the general-equilibrium analysis of trade between regions or countries; for example, Krugman and Venables (1995) explain how manufacturing activities (and hence wealth) are concentrated in the north in a north-south dichotomized world setting. Fujita, Krugman, and Venables (1999), Fujita and Thisse (2002), and Baldwin and others (2003) provide a good synthesis of the model, its variants, and its applications.

3. This is often described in the core-periphery model, a subset of economic geography literature that analyzes how economic activities do or do not concentrate.

4. The concept of backward and forward linkages was first developed by Hirschman (1958). *Backward linkages* exist when increased production by downstream firms provides positive pecuniary externalities to upstream firms. These linkages are "backward" because changes are transmitted back to a previous stage of production. An increase in production by downstream firms generates an increase in demand for upstream firms. *Forward linkages* exist when increased production by upstream firms provides positive pecuniary externalities to downstream firms.

5. Many researchers have discussed the role of network effects in fractionalizing markets in Africa. Using data from Kenya and Zimbabwe, Fafchamps (2000) and Biggs, Raturi, and Srivastava (2002) find no evidence that blacks are disadvantaged in the attribution of bank credit, while an ethnic bias is noticeable in the attribution of supplier credit. Unlike credit from financial institutions, supplier credit relies not on formal collateral, but on trust and reputation. While reducing transaction costs and facilitating information flow among themselves, ethnic networks have a negative impact on other parties, such as indigenous entrepreneurs who are excluded from the network. Biggs and Shah (2006) argue that networks raise the performance of "insiders" and, in the sparse business environments in Africa, have negative consequences for market participation of "outsiders," such as small, indigenous enterprises.

6. Only a few studies have applied rigorous econometric methods to estimate the performance of cluster-based enterprises. For example, Akoten, Otsuka,

and Sonobe (2006) on a shoe cluster in Addis Ababa, Ethiopia, and Akoten and Otsuka (2007) on a garment cluster in Nairobi, Kenya.

7. These clusters include both artisanal clusters in rural areas as well as manufacturing clusters in urban areas populated by informal sector micro enterprises.

8. In the classification of Altenburg and Meyer-Stamer (1999), these clusters would be divided into "advanced mass production" clusters and "clusters of transnational corporations."

9. In her study, McCormick cites the cases of Kamukunji (Nairobi, Kenya) and Suame Magazine (Kumasi, Ghana) as examples of the labor "disabling" effect.

10. In the auto cluster in Durban, South Africa, for example, the training program was targeted to decision makers rather than managers.

11. U.S. consultants also played a major role, helping firms to upgrade their product quality and overcome the threat posed by a U.S. embargo on Sialkot instruments on account of poor quality.

References

Akoten, John, and Keijiro Otsuka. 2007. "From Tailors to Mini-Manufacturers: The Role of Traders in the Transformation of Garment Enterprises in Kenya." *Journal of African Economies* 16 (4): 564–95.

Akoten, John, Keijiro Otsuka, and Tetsushi Sonobe. 2006. "The Development of the Footwear Industry in Ethiopia: How Different Is It from the East Asian Experience?" FASID Discussion Paper, FASID, Tokyo.

Altenburg, Tilman, and Jörg Meyer-Stamer. 1999. "How to Promote Clusters: Policy Experiences from Latin America." *World Development* 27 (9): 1693–713.

Artadi, Elasa, and Xavier Sala-i-Martin. 2004. "The Economic Tragedy of the Twentieth Century: Growth in Africa." In *Africa Competitiveness Report 2004*, ed. Ernesto Hernández-Catá, Klaus Schwab, and Augusto Lopez-Claros. Davos, Switzerland: World Economic Forum.

Aryeetey, Ernest, George Owusu, and Peter Quartey. 2009. "Industrial Clusters and Indigenous Private Sector in Africa: Ghana Case Study." Background technical paper prepared for the study.

Baldwin, Richard, Rikard Forslid, Philippe Martin, Gianmarco Ottaviano, and Frederic Robert-Nicoud. 2003. *Economic Geography and Public Policy*. Princeton, NJ: Princeton University Press.

Biggs, Tyler, Mayank Raturi, and Pradeep Srivastava. 2002. "Ethnic Networks and Access to Credit: Evidence from the Manufacturing Sector in Kenya." *Journal of Economic Behavior and Organization* 49 (4): 473–86.

Biggs, Tyler, and Manju Shah. 2006. "African SMEs, Networks, and Manufacturing Performance." *Journal of Banking and Finance* 30 (11): 3043–66.

Dixit, Avinash, and Joseph E. Stiglitz. 1977. "Monopolistic Competition and Optimum Product Diversity." *American Economic Review* 67 (3): 297–308.

Fafchamps, Marcel. 2000. "Ethnicity and Credit in African Manufacturing." *Journal of Development Economics* 61 (1): 205–36.

Fujita, Masahisa. 2003. "Implications and Issues for Cluster Policies from the Point of View of Spatial Economy [in Japanese]." Research Institute of Economy, Trade, and Industry, Tokyo.

Fujita, Masahisa, Paul Krugman, and Anthony J. Venables. 1999. *The Spatial Economy: Cities, Regions, and International Trade.* Cambridge, MA: MIT Press.

Fujita, Masahisa, and Jacques-François Thisse. 2002. *Economics of Agglomeration: Cities, Industrial Location, and Regional Growth.* Cambridge, U.K.: Cambridge University Press.

Gunning, Jan Willem, and Taye Mengistae. 2001. "Determinants of African Manufacturing Investment: The Microeconomic Evidence." *Journal of African Economies* 10 (supplement 2): 48–80.

Hirschman, Albert O. 1958. *The Strategy of Economic Development.* New Haven, CT: Yale University Press.

Krugman, Paul. 1991. "Increasing Returns and Economic Geography." *Journal of Political Economy* 99 (3): 483–99.

Kuchiki, Akifumi, and Masatsugo Tsuji, eds. 2005. *Industrial Clusters in Asia: Analysis of Their Competition and Cooperation.* New York: Palgrave Macmillan.

Marshall, Alfred. 1920. *Principles of Economics.* London: Macmillan.

McCormick, Dorothy. 1999. "African Enterprise Clusters and Industrialization: Theory and Reality." *World Development* 27 (9): 1531–51.

McPherson, Michael A. 1996. "Growth of Micro and Small Enterprises in Southern Africa." *Journal of Development Economics* 48 (21): 31–54.

Mengistae, Taye. 2006. "Competition and Entrepreneurs' Human Capital in Small Business Longevity and Growth." *Journal of Development Studies* 42 (5): 812–36.

Morosini, Piero. 2004. "Industrial Clusters, Knowledge Integration, and Performance." *World Development* 32 (2): 305–26.

Muto, Megumi, Takuro Takeuchi, and Noribumi Koike. 2007. "Policy Coherence in Development: Case Study of East Asia." Working Paper 24. Japan Bank for International Cooperation, Tokyo (October).

Nadvi, Khalid. 1996. "Small Firm Industrial Districts in Pakistan." D.Phil. thesis, University of Sussex.

———. 1999. "Collective Efficiency and Collective Failure: The Response of the Sialkot Surgical Instrument Cluster to Global Quality Pressures." *World Development* 27 (9): 1605–26.

Oyelaran-Oyeyinka, Banji, and Dorothy McCormick, eds. 2007. *Industrial Clusters and Innovation Systems in Africa.* Tokyo: United Nations University Press.

Pack, Howard, and Kamal Saggi. 2006. "Is There a Case for Industrial Policy? A Critical Survey." *World Bank Research Observer* 21 (2): 267–97.

Porter, Michael E. 1985. *Competitive Advantage.* New York: Free Press.

Ramachandran, Vijaya, Alan Gelb, and Manju Shah. 2009. *Africa's Private Sector: What's Wrong with the Business Environment and What to Do about It.* Washington, DC: Center for Global Development.

Ramachandran, Vijaya, and Manju K. Shah. 1999. "Minority Entrepreneurs and Firm Performance in Sub-Saharan Africa." *Journal of Development Studies* 36 (2): 71–87.

Schmitz, Hubert, and Khalid Nadvi. 1999. "Clustering and Industrialization: Introduction." *World Development* 27 (9): 1503–14.

Sonobe, Tetsushi, and Keijiro Otsuka. 2006a. *Cluster-Based Industrial Development: An East Asian Model.* New York: Palgrave Macmillan.

———. 2006b. "Strategy for Cluster-Based Industrial Development in Developing Countries." Unpublished mss., FASID, Tokyo.

Tewari, Meenu. 1999. "Successful Adjustment in Indian Industry: The Case of Ludhiana's Woolen Knitwear Cluster." *World Development* 27 (9): 1651–71.

Visser, Evert-Jan. 1999. "A Comparison of Clustered and Dispersed Firms in the Small-Scale Clothing Industry in Lima." *World Development* 27 (9): 1553–70.

World Bank. 2009. *Cluster Initiatives for Competitiveness: A Practical Guide and Toolkit.* Washington, DC: World Bank.

Yoshino, Yutaka. 2009. "Industrial Clusters in Developing Countries: A Conceptual Framework from Spatial Economics Perspective." Background analytical note prepared for the study.

Zeng, Douglas Zhihua. 2008. *Knowledge, Technology, and Cluster-Based Growth in Africa.* Washington, DC: World Bank Institute.

CHAPTER 4

Industrial Clusters and Business Performance of Micro and Small Enterprises in Africa

Can industrial clusters provide an environment for micro and small enterprises to improve their businesses? In collaboration with researchers affiliated with the African Economic Research Consortium, the World Bank team conducted case studies of select industrial clusters in five countries in Sub-Saharan Africa—Cameroon, Ghana, Kenya, Mauritius, and Rwanda—and collected quantitative and qualitative data from those clusters.[1] These five countries were selected based on knowledge about the existence of industrial clusters as well as income, geographic, and linguistic variations among countries. In total, 15 clusters were covered from these five countries. Those 15 clusters are presented in table 4.1.[2]

Following the definition of industrial clusters discussed in chapter 3, the clusters covered by the case studies were chosen on the basis of geographic concentration of the same or related industrial or commercial activities, with a focus on spontaneously grown natural industrial clusters. The decision of how narrowly to define geographic concentration varies depending on the geographic setting of the country as well as the industry. In Cameroon, Ghana, Kenya, and Rwanda, all clusters in manufacturing sectors are visible physical concentrations of enterprises located in relatively narrowly defined geographic areas, such as blocks, streets, and

Table 4.1   List of Clusters Covered by the Five-Country Case Studies

Type of cluster and location	Area or group	Firm size range	Industry
a. Light manufacturing industries			
Spontaneous agglomerations of micro and small enterprises in small areas			
Yaoundé, Cameroon	Olézoa	Micro-small	Furniture
Yaoundé, Cameroon	Briqueterie	Micro-small	Textiles and garments
Douala, Cameroon	Bonabéri	Micro	Furniture
Douala, Cameroon	Marché Congo	Micro	Textiles and garments
Kumasi, Ghana	Suame Magazine	Micro-small	Metalwork and machinery
Kumasi, Ghana	Furniture cluster	Micro-small	Furniture
Nairobi, Kenya	Kariobangi Light Industry	Micro-small	Metalwork and machinery
Nairobi, Kenya	Uhuru Market	Micro-small	Garments
Nakuru, Kenya	Canon Street	Small	Furniture
Kigali, Rwanda	Gakinjiro	Micro-small	Metalwork
b. Nonmanufacturing nontraditional clusters			
Value chain–driven clusters of export crops			
Nsawan, Ghana	Suppliers to a pineapple exporter	Small-medium	Pineapple
Butare, Rwanda	Suppliers to a coffee brand	Small-medium	Coffee
IT zones			
Ebena City, Mauritius	Ebena Cyber Tower	Small-medium-large	IT
Kigali, Rwanda	ICT Park		IT
Tourism cluster			
Ruhengeri, Rwanda	Virunga Mountain Gorilla Park	Micro-small	Hotel and restaurant

Source: Authors.

neighborhoods within a city. In most cases, there are no rigidly defined boundaries, but the core areas of these clusters are populated almost exclusively by enterprises engaged in the same or similar productive or commercial activities; by and large they are contiguous to one another. The perceived boundaries of these clusters are usually defined as the outer rim of the continuum of enterprises.[3]

Spontaneously grown natural clusters, mostly populated by micro and small enterprises, are the most common type of cluster in Africa. Some of these started when enterprises settled in a certain location in response to government zoning regulations and policies or other public interventions. Nevertheless, the clusters agglomerated and grew spontaneously. The quantitative analysis in this chapter focuses mostly on such spontaneously grown natural clusters and uses pooled data collected from the case studies on those clusters. The clusters studied were selected from three light manufacturing sectors: metalwork and machinery, furniture, and textiles and garments. These three sectors are the most typical sectors with spontaneously grown natural clusters in Africa, are more represented by micro and small domestic enterprises, and produce products that are relatively exportable to regional markets within Africa, if not to developed economies. In all, 10 industrial clusters in light manufacturing sectors were studied. All 10 are concentrations of enterprises in specific neighborhoods or streets within the capital or a major industrial city.

In addition to spontaneously grown natural clusters in light manufacturing sectors, the case studies also include nontraditional, nonmanufacturing clusters. The nontraditional, nonmanufacturing clusters include agriculture clusters formed by value chain networks of export crops, information technology (IT) clusters in Rwanda and Mauritius, and a tourism cluster in Rwanda. Geographic areas are much larger for agricultural products than for manufacturing products, given that agriculture is more land intensive than manufacturing. In both the pineapple cluster in Ghana and the coffee cluster in Rwanda, clusters are identified as concentrated areas of suppliers (outgrowers) of products connected to a certain exporter or brand. Thus while geographic proximity among outgrowers is weaker for agriculture than for manufacturing clusters, linkages with the same buyers provide the basis for a horizontal network. The data from these clusters are not included in the pooled data analysis because they are so different from the spontaneously grown light manufacturing clusters. Some of those nontraditional clusters were created and developed by explicit government programs to establish industrial parks as in the case of IT clusters by attracting enterprises with incentives such as subsidized rent for plots in the park, space in designated buildings, and access to infrastructure.

Enterprise data were collected both from enterprises sampled inside the clusters and from comparator enterprises, which are located outside the clusters but in the same industry and the same geographic area (for example, a city if the cluster is a concentration at the street or the neighborhood level within the city). Data were collected from approximately 500 enterprises, including those located in 15 clusters (10 light manufacturing clusters and five nontraditional nonmanufacturing clusters) as well as their outside comparators.[4] The majority of clusters in the data set are concentrations of micro and small enterprises owned and managed by domestic African entrepreneurs who are operating in an informal setting. Out of 303 cluster-based enterprises in the sample, 77 percent are considered micro (fewer than five employees) or small (five or more employees, but fewer than 20).[5] About 10 percent of the enterprises in the inside and outside group are owned by foreign nationals.

Clustering and Business Performance: Natural Industrial Clusters in Light Manufacturing Industries

How do cluster-based enterprises perform relative to their comparators outside of the clusters? Using the enterprise data collected from inside and outside the 10 light manufacturing clusters, we analyze how cluster-based enterprises perform with regard to productivity and market expansion compared with outside enterprises.

The basic characteristics of the enterprises studied are presented in appendix 2. The vast majority of enterprises in the data set are owned by males: 84 percent inside and 78 percent outside the clusters. Entrepreneurs inside the clusters tend to have less education than those outside. Inside clusters, 41 percent of entrepreneurs have some university education and 3 percent have a university degree, compared with 52 and 9 percent, respectively, of those outside the clusters.[6]

Productivity

Cluster-based enterprises have higher labor productivity than outside comparators, on average. Enterprises inside the clusters show higher sales per worker, on average, than comparator enterprises in the same city and the same industry, but not in a cluster (see figure 4.1). Cluster-based enterprises are, on average, more capital intensive than their outside comparators, suggesting a correlation between sales performance and capital intensity. Although based on different data sets, the existence of a cluster premium is also observed for value added per worker (see box 4.1).

As in chapter 2, we apply the Blinder-Oaxaca decomposition method to analyze which factors contribute to the difference in productivity between cluster-based enterprises and their outside comparators—the *cluster premium* on productivity. As shown in table 4.2, we analyze, separately for cluster-based enterprises and their outside comparators, how their productivity measured by sales per worker is affected by capital endowment, size, skill level of labor, and manager's education.

Figure 4.1   Differential of Sales per Worker and Capital per Worker Inside and Outside of Spontaneous Light Manufacturing Clusters

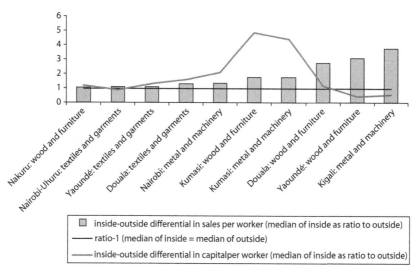

Source: Bougna and Yoshino 2009, based on the data of micro and small enterprises inside the 10 light manufacturing clusters and their outside comparators collected as part of the original five-country case studies of industrial clusters.

Box 4.1

Labor Productivity of Cluster-Based Enterprises and National Averages

Figure B4.1 shows the median value added per worker of enterprises in clusters, based on the original survey data, compared to the median value added per worker of various subsets of enterprises (including both cluster-based and out-side enterprises) in Ghana and Kenya, based on WBES data. The average produc-tivity of enterprises in Suame Magazine is higher than the average productivity of micro and small enterprises in Ghana in general as well as in the metal and machinery sector. In Kariobangi Light Industries in Kenya, cluster-based enter-prises are more productive than micro and small enterprises, on average, in the same industry.

(continued next page)

Box 4.1 *(continued)*

Figure B4.1   Labor Productivity of Cluster-Based Enterprises Compared with the National Average, 2006

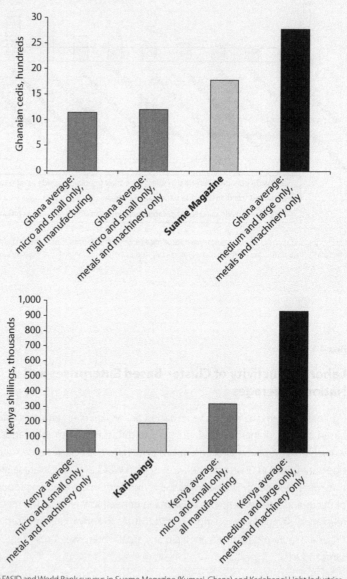

Sources: FASID and World Bank surveys in Suame Magazine (Kumasi, Ghana) and Kariobangi Light Industries (Nairobi, Kenya) in 2008; WBES in Kenya and Ghana in 2007.
Note: All figures are from data provided for 2006 in those surveys.

Table 4.2   Blinder-Oaxaca Decomposition of the Cluster Premium on Productivity
dependent variable = sales per worker (log)

	OLS		Blinder-Oaxaca decomposition (control: located in cluster)		
Independent variable	Inside of cluster	Outside of cluster	Endowment effect	Coefficient effect	Interaction effect
Capital per worker	0.244***	0.213***	0.116**	0.206	−0.015
(log)	(0.055)	(0.073)	(0.049)	(0.613)	(0.044)
Size (dummy: more	−0.376**	−0.182	−0.088*	−0.292	0.046
than 5 workers)	(0.175)	(0.215)	(0.046)	(0.417)	(0.066)
Number of apprentices	−0.086*	−0.074	0.009	−0.014	−0.001
(ratio to permanent	(0.047)	(0.055)	(0.020)	(0.089)	(0.008)
workers)					
Manager's education	−0.0520	0.159	−0.008	−0.088	−0.030
(postsecondary)	(0.182)	(0.201)	(0.027)	(0.113)	(0.041)
Number of					
observations	166	132		298	
R^2	0.322	0.236			

Source: Bougna and Yoshino 2009, based on the data of micro and small enterprises inside the 10 light manufacturing clusters and their outside comparators collected as part of the original five-country case studies of industrial clusters.
Note: Industry, regional, and cluster dummies as well as constant are included but not reported. Standard errors are in parentheses.
*** $p < 0.01$.
** $p < 0.05$.
* $p < 0.10$.

Based on those factors, the cluster-based enterprises are predicted to be 25 percent more productive than outside comparators based on those factors (table 4.3).

Cluster-based enterprises have higher capital endowment than their comparators outside the clusters, and this is the primary source of their higher average productivity. As shown in table 4.2, the principal contributor to the cluster premium is higher capital intensity, as measured by capital per worker among cluster-based enterprises.[7] Cluster-based enterprises have better access to physical capital given the existence in clusters of a second-hand market for machines and tools. When some enterprises buy new machines and tools, they sell their old ones to other enterprises in the cluster.

Enterprises with more workers are less productive partly because their ratio of unskilled apprentices to permanent workers is higher. The pattern is particularly discernible among cluster-based enterprises. The size of enterprises, based on the total number of workers, in the data set is

Table 4.3   Predicted Productivity Level Inside and Outside of Clusters

Location	Predicted sales per worker (log) from OLS
Inside of cluster	7.892***
	(0.089)
Outside of cluster	7.642***
	(0.092)
Differential	0.251*
	(0.128)

Source: Bougna and Yoshino 2009, based on the data of micro and small enterprises inside the 10 light manufacturing clusters and their outside comparators collected as part of the original five-country case studies of industrial clusters.

Note: Predicted level of productivity is estimated by regressing sales per worker (log) on capital per worker (log), size (dummy: more than 5 workers), number of apprentices (ratio to permanent workers), and managers' education (postsecondary). See table 4.2 for coefficient estimates by OLS. Industry, regional, and cluster dummies as well as a constant are included but not reported. Standard errors are in parentheses.

*** $p < 0.01$.

* $p < 0.10$.

inversely correlated with sales per worker, particularly among cluster-based enterprises. This finding is contrary to what is normally observed when large enterprises are included in the analysis. These "diseconomies of scale" are likely a result of the high proportion of unskilled apprentices in the workforce of micro and small enterprises in the data set. In fact, sales performance is negatively associated with the ratio of apprentices to permanent workers, as shown in the significant, negative coefficient for the ratio among cluster-based enterprises.

There is little difference in the educational background of managers and access to finance between cluster-based enterprises and their comparators. Cluster-based enterprises do not necessarily have better access to formal finance than firms outside a cluster. With few exceptions, such as the cluster-based credit union that previously existed in the Gakinjiro cluster in Kigali, Rwanda, clusters have not yet attracted financial services. In Kariobangi Light Industries, several commercial banks have branch offices adjacent to the area of industrial concentration and serve manufacturers in the cluster. However, the services provided by those branches are almost solely for consumer banking, facilitating deposits and transfers for those who work in the cluster (Akoten 2009). Among enterprises surveyed for this study, lack of access to finance is considered a serious business constraint regardless of whether or not they are based in an industrial cluster.

Are cluster-based enterprises more productive because enterprises become more productive in the clusters, or because more productive enterprises choose to be located in the clusters? A simple regression analysis, as above, does not indicate a causal relationship between the location and the productivity level of enterprises in the data set. Therefore, the result does not automatically imply that clustering causes enterprises to have higher productivity. One may argue that the reason for higher average productivity inside the clusters is that more productive enterprises join a cluster. In other words, more productive enterprises self-select to be located in a cluster. This may be the case for formal enterprises located in an industrial zone constructed by the government. Only potentially high-performing enterprises are likely to be admitted to such locations. However, in the case of spontaneously grown natural industrial clusters, such as those observed in the case studies, it does not appear that better performers are attracted to the clusters. Clusters are formed as new enterprises seek to co-locate with highly profitable enterprises. However, potentially productive enterprises would rather not co-locate with existing enterprises in clusters because they would be better off choosing a less congested area and avoiding head-to-head competition with existing enterprises. They would rather choose a location outside of the clusters.

Participation in Nonlocal Markets

The data show that more cluster-based enterprises are selling their products to nonlocal markets and doing so more intensively than outside enterprises. Across-the-board, for all 10 industrial clusters, more cluster-based enterprises participate in selling their products outside the local market, either to national or to international markets, than outside comparators (see figure 4.2). The same applies to sales intensity in nonlocal markets, measured as the percentage of total sales outside of local markets. In most of the clusters, cluster-based enterprises also participate more in export markets, in terms of both participation rate and sales intensity. The strong advantage of cluster-based enterprises in expanding their market share and reaching a wider set of customers is corroborated by the choice of location of cluster-based entrepreneurs. As discussed more in depth in the next chapter, better access to customers is cited as the primary reason for the vast majority of entrepreneurs to be based in a cluster.

Cluster-based enterprises are oriented toward nonlocal markets across the three light manufacturing sectors covered by this study. With regard to the linkages with input markets, cluster-based enterprises tend to purchase more inputs from the local neighborhood, while outside enterprises tend to purchase more from outside neighborhoods in the same city (see figure 4.3). This pattern strongly supports the hypothesis

Figure 4.2   Differential of Market Participation Inside and Outside of Spontaneous Light Manufacturing Clusters

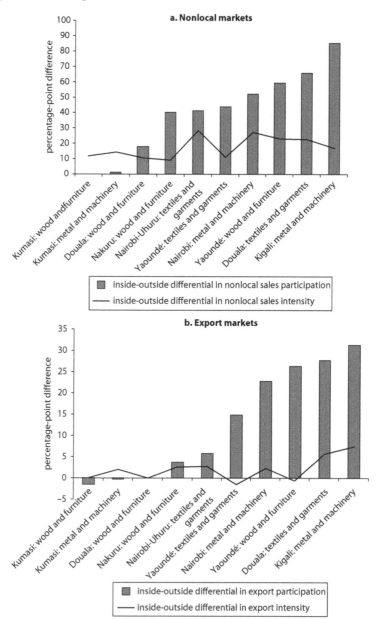

Source: Bougna and Yoshino 2009, based on the data of micro and small enterprises inside the 10 light manufacturing clusters and their outside comparators collected as part of the original five-country case studies of industrial clusters.

Note: Inside-outside percentage-point differential in participation and intensity of sales in nonlocal markets.

Figure 4.3   Distribution of Sales and Purchases, by Location of Buyers and Suppliers

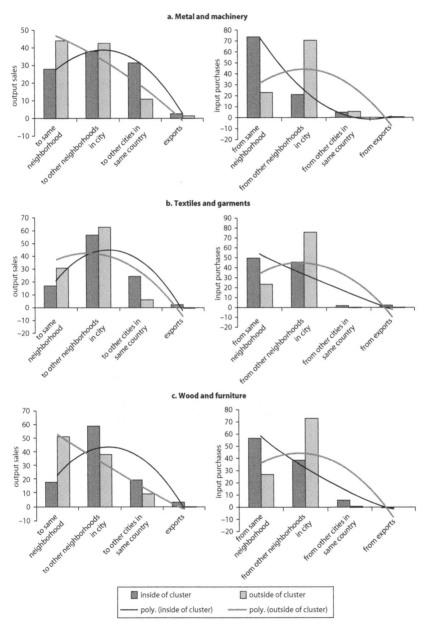

Source: Bougna and Yoshino 2009, based on the data of micro and small enterprises inside the 10 light manufacturing clusters and their outside comparators collected as part of the original five-country case studies of industrial clusters.

that buyer-seller networks are operating within industrial clusters (in the same neighborhoods), while clusters facilitate access to external markets for outputs.

Overall, cluster-based enterprises selling to nonlocal markets tend to interact with other enterprises through commercial transactions and business associations. As shown in figure 4.4, both cluster-based and outside enterprises that participate in nonlocal markets have a strong tendency to sell products to other businesses rather than to end consumers. The pattern is more strongly associated with the market orientation of enterprises (whether or not they participate in nonlocal markets) than with their location (whether or not they are located in a cluster). However, the practice of selling products jointly with other enterprises occurs inside the cluster, but is rare outside, regardless of the market orientation of the enterprise. So the joint sales practice is related more to location than to market orientation. With regard to subcontracting practices—either

Figure 4.4   Rate of Participation in Interfirm Transactions

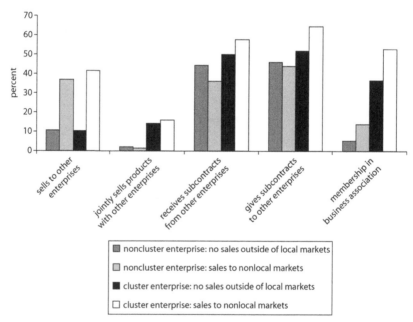

Source: Bougna and Yoshino 2009, based on the data of micro and small enterprises inside the 10 light manufacturing clusters and their outside comparators collected as part of the original five-country case studies of industrial clusters.

receiving subcontracts from other enterprises or giving them to others—the pattern is ambiguous. But the practice appears to be more common inside of clusters than outside, and, among cluster-based enterprises, those that sell outside of their local market are more actively engaged in subcontracting. Membership in a business association is more prevalent among cluster-based enterprises and more prevalent among firms selling to nonlocal markets, showing a correlation with both market orientation and location of the enterprise.

A strong cluster effect on sales participation in nonlocal markets in general and export markets in particular is confirmed in a multivariate analysis. To see how being located in a cluster enhances an enterprise's likelihood of selling its products outside of local markets, we conduct a set of probit model regressions to identify (a) which characteristics, including interfirm transactions, contribute to the probability of selling in nonlocal markets in general and in export markets in particular and (b) how the results change with and without taking into account whether enterprises are inside or outside a cluster. The results of coefficient estimations from the probit model are shown in table 4.4. Figure 4.5 presents the marginal effects in terms of probability. Being

Table 4.4   Probit Model Estimation of Participation in Nonlocal Market Sales and Export Sales

Independent variable	Nonlocal sales (dummy)		Export sales (dummy)	
	Location not controlled	Location controlled	Location not controlled	Location controlled
Located in cluster	n.a.	1.150***	n.a.	0.704***
		(0.216)		(0.240)
Capital per worker (log)	−0.000	−0.051	−0.000	−0.030
	(0.069)	(0.071)	(0.060)	(0.061)
Size (dummy: more than 5 workers)	0.507***	0.300	0.270	0.141
	(0.186)	(0.193)	(0.193)	(0.197)
Number of apprentices (ratio to permanent workers)	−0.056	0.0123	0.058	0.072
	(0.069)	(0.072)	(0.053)	(0.055)
Manager's education (postsecondary)	−0.324	−0.144	0.413**	0.572***
	(0.197)	(0.205)	(0.207)	(0.213)
Giving subcontracts to other enterprises	0.026	0.0945	0.342	0.313
	(0.260)	(0.276)	(0.262)	(0.268)

(continued next page)

Table 4.4   Probit Model Estimation of Participation in Nonlocal Market Sales and Export Sales *(continued)*

Independent variable	Nonlocal sales (dummy)		Export sales (dummy)	
	Location not controlled	*Location controlled*	*Location not controlled*	*Location controlled*
Receiving subcontracts	0.097	0.062	−0.569**	−0.538**
from other enterprises	(0.248)	(0.262)	(0.256)	(0.264)
Selling to other enterprises	0.721***	0.723***	−0.058	−0.118
	(0.226)	(0.233)	(0.215)	(0.224)
Membership in business	0.564**	0.104	0.326	0.024
association	(0.256)	(0.285)	(0.203)	(0.225)
Jointly sold products	0.121	−0.115	0.587*	0.500
	(0.290)	(0.301)	(0.317)	(0.327)
Number of observations	287	287	313	313
R^2	0.2213	0.3024	0.176	0.2044

Source: Bougna and Yoshino 2009, based on the data of micro and small enterprises inside the 10 light manufacturing clusters and their outside comparators collected as part of the original five-country case studies of industrial clusters.
Note: Industry, regional, and cluster dummies as well as constant are included but not reported. Standard errors are in parentheses. n.a. = not applicable.
*** $p < 0.01$.
** $p < 0.05$.
* $p < 0.10$.

located inside a cluster increases the probability of an enterprise selling its products outside the local market by more than 40 percent and the probability of exporting its products by more than 10 percent.

The analysis also shows some practices of interfirm transactions and associations that support enterprises' participation in nonlocal markets, including exports. Enterprises selling their products to other enterprises (business-to-business sales) are 26 percent more likely to sell their products in markets outside of local markets. Business-to-business sales tend to be of larger quantities and based on longer-term contracts than sales to end consumers, therefore improving the incentives for entrepreneurs to sell in distant markets. Enterprises that belong to business associations are 21 percent more likely to sell their products in nonlocal markets. One of the key roles of business associations is to facilitate trade for their members, such as organizing a joint exhibition, a showroom, or a trade fair. Enterprises that sell their products jointly with other enterprises have a 15 percent higher chance of exporting their products. Collaboration among enterprises helps enterprises to split their costs of developing new customers in other countries, thereby reducing some of the fixed costs of exporting. At the same time, enterprises receiving

Figure 4.5   Marginal Effects on Probability of Participating in Nonlocal Market Sales and Export Sales

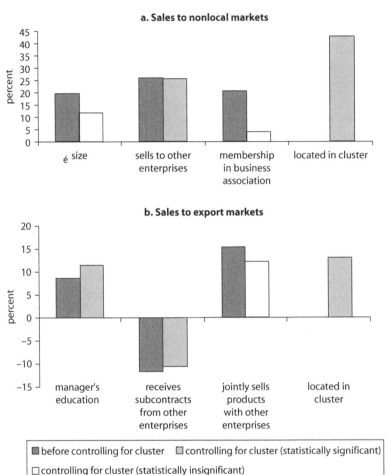

a. Sales to nonlocal markets

b. Sales to export markets

before controlling for cluster   controlling for cluster (statistically significant)
controlling for cluster (statistically insignificant)

Source: Bougna and Yoshino 2009, based on the data of micro and small enterprises inside the 10 light manufacturing clusters and their outside comparators collected as part of the original five-country case studies of industrial clusters.

subcontracts from other enterprises are less likely to export because they support the production of other enterprises that may be exporting rather than engaging in exports themselves.

Some of those interfirm transactions, such as joint sales practice and business association membership, seem to be associated with clustering, explaining why cluster-based enterprises do better in selling to nonlocal markets than enterprises outside of the clusters. Once clustering is controlled for, this factor becomes insignificant, indicating that clustering could play a similar role to that of business associations in facilitating joint marketing of products.[8] For export markets, the practice of joint sales is substituted by clustering, possibly because of the "joint action" mechanism of clusters. This effect, however, becomes weaker and insignificant when clustering is taken into account in the probit model analysis. In fact, a separate probit model analysis suggests that membership in a business association as well as location in a cluster together increase the probability that enterprises sell their products jointly. This underscores the mechanism of "joint actions" in clustering through which cluster-based enterprises collectively develop markets and promote their products, which overlaps with association membership. Such collective actions are particularly important when firms are entering a new market. The joint actions from clustering may be particularly helpful for female entrepreneurs participating in a nonlocal market (see box 4.2).

Box 4.2

Clusters and Gender

The gender balance in the clusters is heavily based on the overall gender balance of the business sector itself. Sectors such as textiles and garments have higher representation of female entrepreneurs than metalwork and machinery. Consequently, among the clusters analyzed in the case studies, men dominate metal-processing clusters, whereas women are more visible in garment and handicraft clusters. Businesses run by women entrepreneurs are dominant in the Nairobi-Uhuru Market, one of the garment clusters covered by the case studies. According to data collected from the case studies, cluster-based enterprises owned by females sell in nonlocal markets relatively more than cluster-based enterprises owned by men and firms owned by women that are located outside of the clusters (see figure B4.2). Female-owned, cluster-based enterprises tend to be more likely to participate in joint sales practices or to be members of a business association. Some clusters in Africa are organized predominantly by female entrepreneurs as a mechanism for forming horizontal business networks. As they become more organized, they may take collective action such as lobbying for public policies to address relevant issues, as some organizations in the garment industry in Ghana do.

Figure B4.2   Characteristics of Firms Inside and Outside Clusters, by Location and Gender of Owner

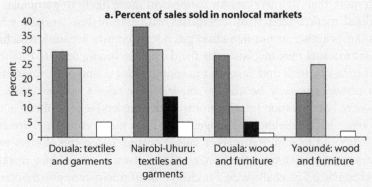

a. Percent of sales sold in nonlocal markets

b. Jointly selling products with other enterprises

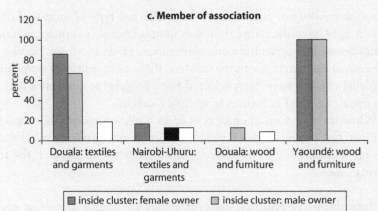

c. Member of association

■ inside cluster: female owner   ▢ inside cluster: male owner
■ outside cluster: female owner   ☐ outside cluster: male owner

Source: Bougna and Yoshino 2009, based on the data of micro and small enterprises inside the 10 light manufacturing clusters and their outside comparators collected as part of the original five-country case studies of industrial clusters.

Clustering seems to provide a size effect for participation in nonlocal markets. Unlike the case of labor productivity, there is a positive scale effect from clustering to participation in nonlocal markets. Enterprises with more than five workers are 20 percent more likely to participate in nonlocal market sales than enterprises with five or less workers when location, whether or not in a cluster, is not taken into account. Reaching distant markets may involve some fixed costs, including costs to establish marketing channels and costs to transport products, and only enterprises of a certain size may be able to expand their sales to distant markets. However, once location (inside or outside the clusters) is controlled for, the difference in the likelihood is insignificant. Even micro enterprises are able to participate in nonlocal market sales. Locating inside the clusters may help enterprises to reduce the fixed costs. For example, establishing marketing channels is less challenging for cluster-based micro enterprises because clusters attract potential customers from outside the local markets.

Some factors continue to be significant in facilitating participation in nonlocal market sales even after controlling for location. Consistent with figure 4.4, engagement in business-to-business sales is a significant factor in facilitating nonlocal market sales regardless of whether the enterprise is located in a cluster or not. Educational background of managers is also significant in facilitating export market sales. This does not change when location is taken into account.

Nontraditional, Nonmanufacturing Clusters in Africa

The case studies not only capture the traditional type of industrial clusters in light manufacturing, but also nontraditional, nonmanufacturing industries such as agriculture and agribusiness, IT, and tourism. Similar to the case of light manufacturing clusters, those nontraditional nonmanufacturing clusters have been selected from geographic concentrations of the same or related industries in specific locations.

While the selection of clusters is again based on geographic concentrations, the implications of geography for nonmanufacturing clusters diverge substantially from those for manufacturing, as show in the following cases:

- *Agriculture.* Agricultural concentrations are found in certain areas within subnational regions or provinces. For example, in Butare, Rwanda, some areas have higher concentrations of washing stations, which are all connected to a specific coffee exporter. In Ghana, a concentration of pineapple growers is found in Nsawan, all of which are supplying their products to a specific pineapple exporter. Thus geographic concentrations are driven by value chain linkages.

- *Information technology.* Concentration of IT enterprises is driven by public policies to attract development of IT industry by establishing industrial parks and providing infrastructure services with subsidized rates.
- *Tourism.* Tourism clusters are usually strongly bound by geography, since it is built around natural endowments available in specific locations such as mountains, lakes, oceans, and historic sites. Market linkages outside of localities are crucial.

Thus the business performance of geography-based clusters is subject to factors that are significantly different among sectors. Clusters in nonmanufacturing sectors often go beyond geographic concentrations. Depending on how clusters are defined, firms outside of the geographic concentrations could also be part of the cluster.

Value Chain–Driven Agribusiness Clusters

Both the Nsawan pineapple cluster in Ghana and the Butare coffee cluster in Rwanda are defined as geographic concentrations of outgrowers that supply the same crop to the same exporters. The clusters have been developed based on the value chains of marketing export crops. In the Butare coffee cluster, the concentration of coffee growers in one area attracts the establishment of processing factories or washing stations and eases access to the government's support and to input supplies, including fertilizers (Musana and Murenzi 2009). However, in both cases, the formulation of clusters was not based purely on commercial considerations because firms were also attracted to the areas to receive external support from donors seeking to support the notion of fair trade.

Cluster-based enterprises are more strongly connected to nonlocal markets. This is expected given the strong ex ante export-oriented nature of clusters. However, in terms of sales performance, the results vary between the two clusters. The Nsawan pineapple cluster in Ghana appears to be quite strong in its performance both in terms of sales per worker and nonlocal market sales vis-à-vis outside enterprises, while the performance of the Butare coffee cluster in Rwanda is not significantly different from that of outside comparators.

The linkages with larger downstream organizations facilitate access to finance among cluster-based enterprises. Members of the Nsawan pineapple cluster appear to enjoy more favorable access to loans and credit from commercial banks than outside firms (Aryeetey, Owusu, and Quartey 2009).

The findings from quantitative analysis do not provide conclusive findings on the superior business performance of cluster-based enterprises as opposed to outside enterprises. In the case of value chain–driven agribusiness clusters, geography-based comparison of inside and outside firms may not be as relevant as it is for light manufacturing. Even though outside outgrowers are not geographically concentrated in any one area, they may be connected to downstream exporters, which facilitates their sales performance.

IT Clusters

The country case studies cover two IT clusters: Ebene Cyber Tower One in Mauritius and ICT Park in Kigali, Rwanda.

- Ebene Cyber Tower One is a 12-story commercial building located in Ebene Cyber City, Mauritius. The integrated building management system was conceived and implemented by a company based in Chennai, India. The reinforced concrete tower, which was completed in only 18 months, is a fully air-conditioned building with a surface area of 42,275 square meters. Situated in a residential zone about 10 kilometers south of Port Louis, the capital of Mauritius, Ebene Cyber Tower One is part of a plan by the Mauritius government to develop information and communications technology (ICT) as a fifth pillar of the nation's economy.

- The Kigali ICT Park was created in early 2006. It is attached to the Rwanda Information Technology Agency and seeks to create a center of innovation amd production as well as an ICT showcase. The ICT Park has taken over Telecom House Complex, situated in the Kacyiru area of the city of Kigali. It has three components: technology production and a showcase for established ICT companies (both local and international), whereby companies are offered office space and other services at minimal cost; an incubator, where great ideas are nurtured and grown into ICT businesses (support services have been put together, including technical, administrative, and legal services and access to venture capital); and a multidisciplinary center of excellence in ICT, where research and development in cutting-edge technologies is conducted. The three components are complementary, and they have been located in the same premises to exploit the synergy between them.

Access to cheap land and space, due to government incentives, is the primary motive for firms' choice of location. Given the nature of the industry, the standard agglomeration story, which is based on physical proximity and savings from reduced transportation costs, does not apply to the IT industry. The availability of cheap land and low rent for offices is the principal reason that enterprises chose their current location.

However, there is significant labor pooling in IT clusters. In Mauritius, the lack of skilled professionals seems to be less binding inside the cluster than outside. This suggests that, while clustering does not necessarily improve access to a larger customer pool (market) given the technological nature of the industry, the labor pooling effect of industrial clusters does apply. In fact, IT entrepreneurs in the agglomerations are also more educated than their outside comparators (Musana and Murenzi 2009): within IT concentrations, 80 percent of entrepreneurs in Mauritius have a university degree compared with 72 percent of entrepreneurs in Kigali. The effect of skilled labor pooling on IT clusters is consistently observed in other countries in Africa and elsewhere in the world (see box 4.3).

Tourism Clusters

The better performance of cluster-based tourism businesses appears to be related to strong external market linkages, supported by foreign ownership. In the tourism cluster in Rwanda, hotels and restaurants inside of the clusters appear to be performing slightly better than those outside in terms of sales per worker (see box 4.4). However, cluster-based enterprises are doing far better than outside enterprises in terms of market linkages. In terms of sales markets—or in the case of tourism, origins of customers—76 percent of cluster-based enterprises succeed in attracting foreign customers, while only 37 percent of outside enterprises succeed in doing so. Cluster-based enterprises also have much better access to input markets outside of the locality (cluster-based enterprises purchase 37 percents of inputs from outside of Musanze, compared with only 9 percent for outside enterprises). This may be related to the fact that cluster-based enterprises have a larger share of foreign ownership (on average 31 percent, compared with 17 percent for outside enterprises).

Tourism clusters are more closely tied to natural endowments of specific locations. And often, potential clusters exist in rural areas. Thus poor conditions in infrastructure, including road connections and

Box 4.3

IT and IT-Enabled Services Clusters in Africa and around the World

Several African countries are emerging exporters of IT services and, in particular, IT-enabled services. For example, in A.T. Kearney's 2009 global services location index—a semiannual ranking of countries based on their perceived attractiveness as a hub of services outsourcing—the Arab Republic of Egypt ranked 6, Ghana ranked 15, Tunisia ranked 17, Mauritius ranked 25, and Senegal ranked 26. Attracted by an inexpensive, highly educated, and language-proficient workforce, domestic entrepreneurs and foreign multinationals alike are establishing export-oriented businesses to service markets in industrial countries. African exports of IT-enabled services are expected to grow rapidly as the continent becomes increasingly integrated in global ICT networks, boosting Internet broadband capacity and reducing prices.

IT companies have a strong tendency to agglomerate: IT is a knowledge-intensive industry, and companies locate in close proximity to centers of higher education in metropolitan areas with access to electricity, ICT infrastructure, and international transport networks. For example, Egypt hosts a Smart Village Business Park with modern infrastructure outside Cairo, and global leaders such as Hewlett Packard, IBM, Infosys, Microsoft, Oracle, and Wipro have hubs in Cairo that develop software applications and provide technical support to foreign markets. The Egyptian government encourages companies not only by facilitating investments in the removal of infrastructure bottlenecks but also by enhancing the business environment: for example, it recently streamlined administrative procedures for registering a company from four months to less than three days. Ghana's IT-enabled services industry enjoys access to several new public and private training institutes, favorable expatriate amenities, incubation facilities, and active support by the Ghana Software and Services Association (Gasscom). Ghana's IT-enabled services cluster will grow stronger as it develops more professional recruitment and real estate agencies as well as more training programs specifically geared to IT-enabled services.

Attracting strategic anchor investors to gain the critical mass necessary for dynamic cluster effects is a key priority for proactive governments seeking to promote local IT services and IT-enabled services industries. Many countries with underdeveloped infrastructure have also established IT parks to cluster businesses and ease the provision of infrastructure services. The success of the Stanford

Industrial Park (Silicon Valley) in the United States, the Multimedia Super Corridor in Malaysia, the Dalian Tiandi Software Hub in China, and the CasaShore Zone in Morocco are examples of policy-induced efforts to generate dynamic clusters. The government of Kenya announced in 2008 that it will develop a technology park with capacity for 5,000 workers. The Software Parks of India helped to establish IT services and IT-enabled services industries with an estimated US$47 billion worth of exports in 2009, 95 percent of which is provided by seven city clusters.

Sources: Michael Engman contributed to this box. A. T. Kearney 2009; Dongier and Sudan 2009; Engman 2009; Hewitt Associates 2006; www.nasscom.org.

Box 4.4

Tourism Cluster in Rwanda

The tourism industry in Rwanda is only moderately developed, but it has experienced a revival since 2002. This growth followed the adoption of the new Rwanda Tourism Strategy and the designation of tourism as a priority sector in October 2002. With the country's Vision 2020, tourism has played a larger role in the economy and received greater government support. However, the industry is hampered by weak supporting infrastructure, such as roads and power.

A tourism cluster has developed around Virunga Park in Musanze, which is Rwanda's most mountainous district, containing a large number of volcanoes and a national park. Musanze's main town, Ruhengeri, is one of the largest towns in Rwanda and a tourist hub. Tourist attractions include mountain gorillas (the rarest species in the world), volcanic mountains within the Virunga chain, flora and fauna, Ruhondo Lake covering about 28 square kilometers, Virunga National Park covering about 60 kilometers, and cultural houses in Kinigi. The cluster is small, but growing, and includes hotels, restaurants, and transport services (rental car businesses). Supportive industries such as the handicraft sector and the financial sector are also involved in the cluster. Those businesses are all small to medium-size firms.

Source: Musana and Murenzi 2009.

utilities, bind cluster-based tourism enterprises particularly seriously. In the case of Ruhengeri, cluster-based enterprises face more severe problems with power supply than their outside comparators (Musana and Murenzi 2009).

Notes

1. The data collection and initial analysis were led by Sunday Khan (University of Yaounde II) for Cameroon, Peter Quartey and George Owufu (Institute of Statistical Social and Economic Research) for Ghana, John Akoten (Institute of Policy Analysis and Research Kenya) for Kenya, Vinaye Ancharaz (University of Mauritius) for Mauritius, and Serge Musana (Institute of Policy Analysis and Research Rwanda) for Rwanda. The enterprises were randomly sampled based on the list of enterprises supplied by cluster associations. If such a list did not exist, the aerial sampling method was used.

2. Enterprise data were also collected from two other clusters: a furniture cluster in Gakinjiro in Kigali, Rwanda, and a footwear cluster in Mauritius. The data from those two clusters are not incorporated in the analysis because the number of observations in each cluster is very small.

3. Some cluster-affiliated enterprises can be located outside such natural boundaries, but still be physically close enough to be considered within a cluster and be linked with enterprises inside the boundaries through membership in the same industrial association.

4. The comparator enterprises were selected by stratification at the neighborhood level, and the aerial sampling method was applied in the same city, but in the areas outside of any particular industrial concentration.

5. Since comparator enterprises outside the cluster were chosen to mirror the characteristics of enterprises inside the cluster, the proportion of outside enterprises that are micro and small in size is similar (80 percent).

6. Managers in our data, on average, have weaker educational backgrounds than small-scale enterprises in the World Bank Enterprise Survey (WBES) data for those five countries (61 and 18 percent for postsecondary and university education, respectively). This is presumably a result of the higher representation of micro enterprises in our data compared to WBES data.

7. Capital endowment is measured by the replacement cost of machinery and equipment, which is the standard measure of capital endowment in investment climate assessment reports in Africa. This is a better valuation of capital than book value, particularly for firms that use second-hand machinery and do not keep proper accounts, such as the majority of enterprises captured in the data.

8. Business associations and industrial clusters do not necessarily overlap perfectly, particularly in the context of the 10 light manufacturing industrial

clusters, which are defined narrowly as being within a specific neighborhood within a city. Business associations are usually formed at much wider geographic levels, such as national, provincial, or municipal levels. Some industrial clusters do have cluster-based associations, but some do not. Some clusters have more than one association, differentiated by specific subsectors such as garages and metalwork or professions such as machinists and carpenters.

References

Akoten, John. 2009. "Industrial Clusters and Indigenous Private Sector in Africa: The Case of Kenya." Background technical paper prepared for the study.

Aryeetey, Ernest, George Owusu, and Peter Quartey. 2009. "Industrial Clusters and Indigenous Private Sector in Africa: Ghana Case Study." Background technical paper prepared for the study.

A. T. Kearney. 2009. The Shifting Geography of Offshoring: The 2009 A. T. Kearney Global Services Index. Available online at www.atkearney.com

Bougna, Theophile, and Yutaka Yoshino. 2009. "Industrial Clusters and Micro- and Small Light Manufacturing Enterprises in Africa: Findings from Country Case Studies." Analytical background note prepared for the study.

Dongier, Phillipe, and Randeep Sudom. 2009. "Realizing the Opportunities Presented by the Global Trade in IT-Based Services." In *Information and Communications in Development 2009: Extending Reach and Increasing Impact*, 103-22. Washington, DC: World Bank.

Hewitt Associates. 2006. Improving Business Competitiveness and Increasing Economic Growth in Ghana: The Role of Information and Communications Technologies.

Musana, Serge, and Ivan Murenzi. 2009. "Industrial Clusters and Indigenous Private Sector in Africa: The Case of Rwanda." Background technical paper prepared for the study.

CHAPTER 5

Location, Market Access, and Business Performance of Cluster-Based Enterprises

Chapter 4 discusses the business performance of cluster-based micro and small enterprises on the basis of the data collected from select industrial clusters in Africa, comparing them with enterprises in the same industries and cities but outside a physical concentration. The results show the presence of cluster premiums, both on productivity and on participation in nonlocal markets, as far as micro and small light manufacturing enterprises are concerned. While chapter 4 investigates how natural clustering is quantitatively associated with higher levels of productivity and participation in nonlocal markets in a cross-sectional sense, it is equally important to discuss the dynamic aspects of cluster development and firm behavior in order to have a better understanding of the growth of those natural industrial clusters and the challenges facing cluster-based micro and small enterprises.

This chapter discusses how micro and small light manufacturing enterprises choose their location in relation to clusters—both whether or not they join a cluster as well as where they are located within one—and how their choice of location affects their business performance. In doing so, we use the same data presented in chapter 4, which are from the original five-country case studies of clusters conducted by the World Bank and researchers affiliated with the African Economic Research Consortium, supplemented by the case study of the Arusha furniture cluster in Tanzania conducted by the Japan International Cooperation Agency (JICA). Since no comprehensive data set systematically covers this spectrum of issues, the discussion in this chapter is based on several data sets.

Location Choice of Micro and Small Light Manufacturers

The principal motive of cluster-based entrepreneurs in choosing their location is to secure better market access. In data from the five-country case studies of light manufacturing clusters, almost two-thirds of the owners inside of the select industrial clusters stated that the primary reason for their choice of location is access to markets, either customers for their products or suppliers of inputs (see table 5.1). This is in contrast to

Table 5.1   Top Reason for Choosing Current Location

Reason given	Inside of clusters	Outside of clusters
Factor access		
Easier to find qualified worker	3.1	6.5
Easier to find potential lenders	0.0	0.6
Total for factor access reasons	3.1	7.1
Land and power supply		
Cheaper price or rent for land and building	16.8	18.8
Larger land and building available	13.1	22.1
Better power supply from public grid	1.0	1.9
Total for land and power supply reasons	30.9	42.8
Market access		
Easier to reach new customers from wider geographic areas	40.3	24.7
Closer to where potential customers are located	18.3	14.9
Easier to reach new suppliers of material inputs in wider geographic areas	1.6	1.3
Closer to where potential suppliers of material inputs are located	1.0	0.6
Better road condition to access buyers and suppliers	1.6	2.6
Total for market access reasons	62.8	44.1
Other		
Safer neighborhood	1.6	3.9
Better opportunity for business training	1.0	0.0
Other	0.5	1.9
Total for other reasons	3.1	5.8

Source: Bougna and Yoshino 2009, based on the data of micro and small enterprises inside the 10 light manufacturing clusters and their outside comparators collected as part of the original five-country case studies of industrial clusters.

outside enterprises, for which cost and availability of land and buildings are as important as market access in explaining their current location. Given the cluster premium on market expansion, as discussed in chapter 4, it is understandable that enterprises are attracted to clusters because of their enhanced accessibility to geographically wider sales areas.

Locations that attract more customers are more important than locations that are close to customers. For enterprises keen on accessibility of markets both inside and outside of the clusters, access to sales markets (customers) appears to be more significant than accessibility to suppliers of inputs. For cluster-based enterprises in particular, locations that allow enterprises to attract customers from a wider geographic area are more important than simple physical proximity to customers. Rather than moving to where the customers are, enterprises choose to be located where customers can easily come. This is quite intuitive if we consider a case where enterprises would prefer to set up a workshop close to a major road rather than in the middle of a residential area or office district. Spontaneously grown industrial clusters are mostly located where there is relatively easy access to road networks.

Access to markets is also a primary factor for considering relocation to an alternative location. Not all enterprises are satisfied with their current location, and many indicated that they would move to a different location if given the chance (see table 5.2). Both inside and outside the

Table 5.2   Top Reason for Wanting to Move to New Location, by Reason for Choosing Current Location

% of respondents giving the reason

Reason for choosing current location	Reason for wanting to move to a new location				
	Factor	Land	Market	Other	Total
Inside of clusters					
Factor	0.0	0.0	0.0	2.9	2.9
Land	0.0	4.3	18.8	7.2	30.3
Market	1.4	15.9	34.8	8.7	60.8
Other	0.0	0.0	1.4	4.3	5.7
Total	1.4	20.2	55.0	23.1	99.7
Outside of clusters					
Factor	1.7	1.7	1.7	0.0	5.1
Land	0.0	3.4	20.3	13.6	37.3
Market	5.1	5.1	30.5	8.5	49.2
Other	0.0	1.7	5.1	1.7	8.5
Total	6.8	11.9	57.6	23.8	100.1

Source: Bougna and Yoshino 2009, based on the data of micro and small enterprises inside the 10 light manufacturing clusters and their outside comparators collected as part of the original five-country case studies of industrial clusters.

clusters, more than 30 percent of enterprises would prefer to move to a new location. The majority of cluster-based enterprises preferring to move said that they would seek better accessibility to potential customers (55 percent). Some of those (35 percent) chose their current location based on better access to customers, which implies a strong motivation to expand their markets further by moving to alternative locations. A few enterprises showed interest in securing better access to land and building facilities. This motive appears to be stronger among cluster-based enterprises than outside enterprises, particularly among those who chose their current location based on market access. This observation suggests a possible shortage of land and building facilities inside the current industrial cluster.

Micro-Level Choice of Location and Business Performance: Findings from the Arusha Furniture Cluster Case Study

New entry to clusters is the most obvious mechanism for cluster growth. While the above data show how entrepreneurs describe their locational preferences ex post and their preferences for alternative locations, how do entrepreneurs actually choose their specific location at a more micro level? Choice of location at a very micro level—for example, how individual entrepreneurs choose a specific location within a cluster—would reveal more implicit reasons for agglomerations in addition to explicit economic reasons, as discussed above. In this context, JICA's case study on the Arusha furniture cluster in Tanzania, which comprises several subclusters within the main cluster, provides insights on how informal social networks, such as ethnic networks, and market accessibility help enterprises to choose their specific location within a cluster and how the choice of a specific location affects their productivity.

In the view of economic geography, existing concentrations of enterprises or density of economic activities should attract further entrants. At the same time, previous studies emphasize that African entrepreneurs prefer doing business with members of their own ethnic group because this helps them to lower the otherwise high transaction costs from market failures (see chapter 3). As a result of network externalities along ethnic lines, market entry is easier for members of a particular group, who can be recommended to established firms of the same group (Fafchamps 2000). Other studies suggest that clusters can complement the market by providing positive externalities, including (1) information spillovers,

(2) specialization and division of labor among firms, and (3) development of skilled labor markets (Sonobe and Otsuka 2006). This is particularly relevant in African markets where transaction costs are high. Therefore, as a potential determinant of the choice of location and productivity of firms, it would be interesting to know how ethnicity, which explains network effects, and density, which explains cluster effects, interplay in influencing the choice of location of micro enterprises and how that decision affects their business performance.

In 2007 JICA conducted a door-to-door census of micro and small workshops in the wooden furniture industry in Arusha, Tanzania, which experienced a wave of new entries in the 2005–07 period (which is described in box 5.1).

Ethnic networks facilitate the initial choice of location of new entrants. A conditional logit model is used to understand the factors behind an entrepreneur's decision to set up a workshop in a specific subcluster. The results are shown in table 5.3. A set of workshop characteristics and subcluster characteristics is considered.[1] Furniture workshops choose to locate in the subcluster where the workshops of owners from the same ethnic group are located. New entrants may make this decision because they perceive that ethnic networks provide a higher probability of finding premises for their operations as well as getting introduced to a wood-processing workshop. The result is consistent with the hypothesis that ethnic networks predict subcluster choice of furniture workshops within the cluster.

Thickness of the market attracts new entrants, but not necessarily the physical density. Furniture workshops may choose to locate in subclusters where density, measured by the number of furniture workshops per kilometer, is lower. This is contrary to the prediction from economic geography of clusters that density attracts further entrants. Entrepreneurs instead choose to avoid densely populated subclusters. Rather, the owners of workshops tend to locate where the market is large or where customers are expanding. Customers are expanding along the international road, which is connected to the Kenyan road network or along the road that connects Arusha with inland urban centers. This is consistent with the empirical results of LaFountain (2005) using U.S. data. It may be reasonable to argue that information spillover and sharing of labor markets are occurring at the cluster level. Then, in choosing among subclusters, a balance between seeking proximity to customers while avoiding physical congestion is the rational choice of new entrants. In fact, the increase in demand comes from the fast pace of urbanization and increase in traffic.[2]

Box 5.1

Subclusters within the Arusha Furniture Cluster in Tanzania

The furniture sector in Arusha, Tanzania, has grown rapidly in recent years (see figure B5.1), with a wave of new entrants in 2005–07. The 234 furniture enterprises in our sample are located in five subclusters of Arusha Municipality: 77 are located in Nairobi-Moshi Road Area, 45 in Dodoma-Oljoro Road, 44 in City Center, 38 in Industrial Area, and 30 in Sokoine Road–Arusha Tech.

Figure B5.1   Number of Firms in the Arusha Furniture Cluster, Tanzania, 1980–2007, by Year Established

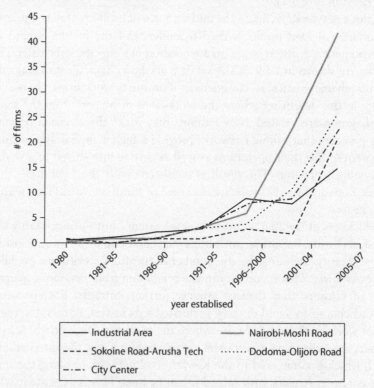

Source: Muto, Chung, and Shimokoshi 2009.

Nairobi-Moshi Road Area refers to a subcluster along the international road from Moshi to Nairobi. Beyond Moshi, it is connected with Dar es Salaam, the capital of Tanzania.

Among the main roads around Arusha Municipality, it is the road with the most traffic. This is the area with the largest number of workshops, 48 percent of them owned by the Chagga ethnic group. The largest number of entrants in 2004–07, the largest number of workshops with a motorized processing machine, and the shortest waiting time for wood processing were in this subsector.

Dodoma–Oljoro Road refers to a subcluster that stretches along the Dodoma Road that connects Arusha Municipality with the central inland area of Tanzania. This area attracts customers from newly developed residential areas within Arusha Municipality as well as from rural towns in inland Tanzania. This subcluster had the second highest number of entrants in 2004–07.

City Center refers to a subcluster around the old city center market, with small-scale workshops scattered within residential and commercial areas.

Industrial Area refers to the subcluster around the industrial zone previously constructed by the government near the old rail station. The industrial zone hosts a variety of industries, from food processing to chemicals. Some large furniture workshops are located on sizable lots, while many new workshops find their place in small corners. The subcluster does not face directly onto a main road, but the road network within the subcluster and access to the main road are good. This subcluster had relatively high frequencies of order sharing and labor sharing between workshops and the highest percentage of workshops accepting install-ment payments as opposed to cash in advance.

Sokoine Road–Arusha Tech refers to the subcluster connecting a corner of Nairobi–Moshi Road (an international road) with Sokoine Road (a main road pass-ing the center of Arusha Municipality). This area attracts customers using both Nairobi-Moshi Road and Sokoine Road, and it is the subcluster that was most densely populated with furniture workshops in 2007. It had the highest percent-age of workshops using the cash in advance method and the longest waiting time for wood processing.

Source: Muto, Chung, and Shimokoshi 2009.

It seems rational for new entrants to choose a subcluster where potential new customers are expanding and where land is still abundant.

We then assess the performance of a workshop, measured by two indi-cators: total efficiency and product quality. Total efficiency is measured by data envelopment analysis and further decomposed into two effi-ciency components: technical efficiency and allocative efficiency (see appendix 3). The level of technical efficiency is extremely low in the

Table 5.3   Determinants of Choice of Subcluster Location in the Arusha Furniture Cluster

Specification	(1)	(2)	(3)	(4)	(5)
Density[a]	−0.07*	−0.05	−0.08	−0.11*	−0.11*
	(−1.88)	(−1.08)	(−1.53)	(−1.87)	(−1.87)
% of own ethnicity	7.13***	7.29***	7.9***	7.52***	7.52***
	(3.22)	(3.14)	(3.30)	(3.00)	(3.00)
Market size[a]		0.56***	0.37*	0.53**	0.53**
		(3.29)	(1.72)	(2.03)	(2.03)
Number of visitors[a]			−0.55	−0.64	−0.64
			(−1.34)	(−1.55)	(−1.55)
Access to timber (driving time)[a]				−0.27	−0.27
				(−1.09)	(−1.09)
Number of observations	640	640	640	640	640

Source: Muto, Chung, and Shimokoshi 2009.
Note: Robust z statistics are in parentheses.
a. 2004.
*** $p < 0.01$.
** $p < 0.05$.
* $p < 0.10$.

Arusha furniture cluster.[3] Product quality is measured by the dryness of the timber used in furniture, information collected at each workshop during the census survey in 2007.

Table 5.4 shows the results of a simple ordinary least squares regression with subcluster dummies on cost efficiency. In terms of workshop characteristics, the number of years of experience of the most experienced worker affects technical efficiency negatively, but affects allocative efficiency positively. The workshop's number of years in operation affects technical efficiency negatively. The volume of production at the workshop level affects technical efficiency positively, suggesting the existence of economies of scale in achieving better performance.

Among subcluster characteristics, co-location with workshops owned by same-ethnicity entrepreneurs does not seem to matter for performance. This is the case for both the total efficiency of their operations and the quality of their products. As for density, allocative efficiency is negatively affected by the density of the subcluster. This suggests some negative externality in subclusters with densely populated workshops.

While ethnic networks facilitate the initial choice of location, actual business performance, with regard to both efficiency and quality of

Table 5.4   Determinants of Performance in the Arusha Furniture Cluster

Variable	Total efficiency	Technical efficiency	Allocative efficiency	Quality: dryness of wood
Age of owner	0.03	−0.01	0.00	0.024
	(0.65)	(−0.93)	(0.01)	(0.97)
Age of owner, squared	0.00	0.00	0.00	0.00
	(−0.60)	(1.18)	(−0.56)	(−0.89)
Previous furniture sales	−0.08**	−0.07*	−0.16**	0.24**
	(−2.09)	(−1.66)	(−2.25)	(2.20)
Furniture maker before	−0.04*	−0.05*	0.06	0.12**
(dummy)	(−1.93)	(−1.68)	(0.97)	(2.08)
Manager's primary school	0.01	0.02	−0.1**	0.07
education	(−0.58)	0.79)	(−1.97)	(1.56)
Production training	0.0003	0.0008	−0.023	0.08
	(0.03)	(−0.05)	(−0.65)	(1.55)
% of own ethnicity	−0.05	−0.035	−0.006	0.07
	(−1.50)	(−0.93)	(−0.07)	(0.58)
Years of experience of	−0.001	−0.003**	0.005*	−0.005
skilled worker	(−0.81)	(−2.11)	(1.86)	(−1.41)
Years in operation	−0.004**	−0.06***	0.001	−0.006
	(−2.28)	(−3.14)	(0.24)	(−0.64)
Amount of production	0.063***	0.095***	−0.01	0.01
of each enterprise	(5.33)	(8.23)	(−0.63)	(0.46)
Equipment	−0.01	0.02	−0.01	0.09*
	(−0.46)	(0.65)	(−0.63)	(1.73)
Amount of production in	0.013	0.029	−0.01	−0.08
the subcluster	(0.72)	(1.34)	(−0.16)	(−1.10)
Wood-processing waiting	−0.003**	−0.002	0.04	−0.02*
time	(−2.41)	(1.60)–	(0.89)	(−1.87)
Density	−0.002	−0.001	−0.13***	0.0003
	(−1.57)	(−0.93)	(−2.94)	(0.06)
Number of observations	215	215	215	219
R^2	0.37	0.52	0.15	0.1

Source: Muto, Chung, and Shimokoshi 2009.
Note: Robust z statistics are in parentheses.
*** $p < 0.01$.
** $p < 0.05$.
* $p < 0.10$.

products, is influenced more by the geographic condition for value chain linkages. Wood-processing waiting time is negatively associated with allocative efficiency and product quality. This suggests that upstream supporting activity in the value chain of furniture production is crucial to the performance of furniture workshops in Arusha Municipality. While ethnicity becomes insignificant in explaining the level of performance, total efficiency and product quality of a furniture workshop are higher in subclusters where the waiting time for wood processing is shorter. These results suggest that, while the network effect is important for the choice of subcluster location, higher performance is observed for workshops that are located in a subcluster where the upstream wood-processing linkage is efficient.

Notes

1. Subcluster characteristics are taken from the survey data collected in 2004 prior to the rapid influx of new entrants.
2. This could be the result of urbanization economies as opposed to localization economies, as in the case of large metropolitan areas studied by Chakravorty, Koo, and Lall (2003). See chapter 6 for more discussion.
3. Overall, the average cost efficiency is 0.102, where average technical efficiency is 0.156 and allocative efficiency is 0.68. The value of 1 indicates that the firm is efficient. Therefore, technical efficiency of 0.156 is extremely low, suggesting that furniture workshops in Arusha do not use inputs efficiently in producing furniture products. Of 226 enterprises, only one enterprise is considered cost-efficient. This enterprise is located in Industry Area.

References

Bougna, Theophile, and Yutaka Yoshino. 2009. "Industrial Clusters and Micro- and Small Light Manufacturing Enterprises in Africa: Findings from Country Case Studies." Analytical background note prepared for the study.

Chakravorty, Sanjoy, Jun Koo, and Somik V. Lall. 2003. "Metropolitan Industrial Clusters Patterns and Processes." Policy Research Working Paper 3073, World Bank, Washington, DC.

Fafchamps, Marcel. 2000. "Ethnicity and Credit in African Manufacturing." *Journal of Development Economics* 61 (1): 205–36.

LaFountain, Courtney. 2005. "Where Do Firms Locate? Testing Competing Models of Agglomeration." *Journal of Urban Economics* 58 (2): 338–66.

Muto, Megumi, Yessica C. Y. Chung, and Shinobu Shimokoshi. 2009. "Location Choice and the Performance of Furniture Workshops in Arusha, Tanzania." Background analytical note prepared for the study.

Sonobe, Tetsushi, and Keijiro Otsuka. 2006. *Cluster-Based Industrial Development: An East Asian Model.* New York: Palgrave Macmillan.

CHAPTER 6

Agglomeration and Growth Challenges for Enterprises in Survival Clusters in Africa

Agglomeration induces more competition and lowers profitability inside of clusters. The presence of a cluster premium on business performance attracts new enterprises to clusters, generating further agglomeration. As shown vividly in figure 6.1 for Suame Magazine, new entrants to the cluster place downward pressure on the profitability of average firms within the cluster as the level of competition grows. The more homogeneous the products are, the more likely it is that the increase in the number of firms in the cluster will directly affect their profit margin. Unless entrepreneurs know how to find new markets, an increase in the number of competitors will result in smaller sales per enterprise and a smaller profit margin.

While increased internal competition is the primary reason for the reduction in profit margin, several additional factors potentially contribute to the decline in profitability from the entrance of new enterprises.

- New entrants are likely to be less productive than incumbents, given that most entrants are spinoffs by the graduating apprentices of existing firms and still have limited capacity.
- As in Suame Magazine, masters seek to discourage graduating apprentices from becoming competitors by raising their salary and keeping them employed in the original workshop. As seen in chapter 4, a high

Figure 6.1   Average Business Performance and Number of Metalwork Enterprises in Suame Magazine, 2000–04

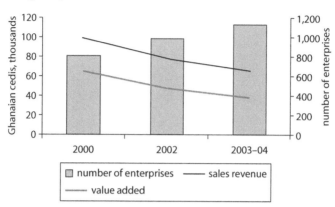

Source: Iddrisu, Mano, and Sonobe 2009.

ratio of apprentices to workers is negatively associated with productivity. Together with the rising costs of metal in Suame Magazine—the result of high demand from China and India for scrap metal—higher labor costs further reduce the profitability of enterprises in the cluster.

• Limited availability of land raises the cost of renting a plot in the cluster and reduces operational efficiency as physical congestion increases within the cluster. This situation is common in many clusters in Africa, including Suame Magazine and Arusha furniture cluster, as discussed in chapter 5. Density does not necessarily have a positive effect on workshop performance.

Cluster-based entrepreneurs are especially sensitive to location-related issues. Given physical proximity among enterprises inside an industrial cluster, maintaining a good and stable internal business environment is critical for the growth of the cluster. Based on the perceptions of investment climate constraints collected as part of the five-country case studies, micro and small light manufacturing enterprises inside an industrial cluster have relatively severe problems related to the business environment, such as crime, unfair competition, and access to land (see figure 6.2). The increased concentration of enterprises produces negative externalities of congestion, worsening the work environment. The Olezoa furniture cluster in Yaoundé, Cameroon, shows how the lack of storage space forces micro

Figure 6.2   Differential in Severity of Investment Climate Constraints among Cluster-based and Outside Enterprises

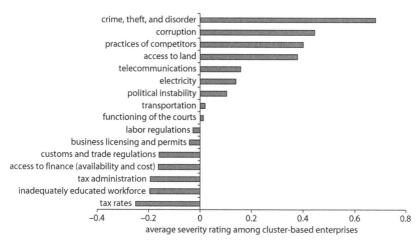

average severity rating among cluster-based enterprises

Source: Bougna and Yoshino 2009, based on the data of micro and small enterprises inside the 10 light manufacturing clusters and their outside comparators collected as part of the original five-country case studies of industrial clusters.
Note: Enterprises were asked to rate the severity of various investment constraints based on a 1-to-5 scale, with 1 being the least severe (no obstacle) and 5 being the most severe (very severe obstacle). The average severity rating among cluster-based enterprises differs from the average severity rating among outside enterprises.

enterprises to purchase small amounts of inputs as they receive orders rather than to stock a large amount of inputs (see box 6.1).

Growth Bottlenecks in Survival Clusters

Increased competition and downward pressure on profit margins contribute to economic efficiency. The question is whether competition is opening up a growth path both for enterprises based in such clusters and for the clusters themselves. Is competition sorting out good performers and forcing out bad performers within clusters? Two structural issues concerning industrial clusters are relevant to this question. How do enterprises compete in the clusters? And is there an effective exit mechanism for enterprises wishing to leave a cluster? Bottlenecks to growth can come from lack of innovation and product differentiation or from lack of spatial mobility. This section deals with each in turn.

Lack of Innovation and Product Differentiation
The naturally formed industrial clusters in Africa are still largely at an early "survival" stage, where cluster formation simply leads to an increased

Box 6.1

The Olezoa Furniture Cluster in Yaoundé

The Olezoa furniture cluster was started in 1993 by Vincent Buma, when the present site was a bushy area. He began by producing furniture and transporting it to Marché Mondial (no longer in existence), where a furniture market had developed. As his business grew, he brought in relatives from the northwest, his region of origin. These relatives eventually brought in other relatives and friends, and the site soon became not only an important production site, but also a well-known furniture market in the city. The cluster has since grown and is reported to have about 150 firms and about 1,000 workers, including firm owners, employees, and apprentices. It runs about 1.5 kilometers along a street, from Prestige Hotel to Trois Status.

The cluster has attracted many other specialized intermediate inputs and service providers. Prominent among them are sawmills. These sawmills are essential for the work of furniture producers, but their cost and capacity are too high for individual ownership. A typical furniture maker does not use the sawmill every day, and even when he uses it, a few hours are enough to satisfy his needs. The market for the main raw material—timber—is just 3 kilometers from the cluster at Messa. Most of the firms buy timber as it is required. They do not store it. Their limited capital and lack of storage space does not permit them to buy timber in large quantities.

Source: Khan 2009.

quantity of production, but not necessarily to improved product quality through innovation and product differentiation. The case of Arusha furniture cluster discussed in chapter 5 finds that economies of scale enable cluster-based enterprises to produce more furniture pieces, but the absolute level of cost efficiency is still extremely low. The enhanced performance based simply on scale may work when market demand does not have a strong taste for quality. However, as the population of Arusha Municipality and other rural towns in Tanzania grows, consumers may start demanding more variety and higher-quality products at a lower cost than before. At that stage, it is unclear how the growth strategy for a furniture workshop will change. Particularly as Arusha improves its road connectivity with other major cities in Tanzania and Kenya and enhanced information technology allows easier flow of market information from other cities, customers may start searching within a wider market sphere. In such a context, it is unclear whether the Arusha furniture cluster will be able to keep its customers in the future.

Clusters in Africa are quite different from the more advanced, innovation-oriented clusters seen elsewhere in the world, where clustering generates innovation and enterprises compete by differentiating their products from those of their competitors. Enterprises that succeed in innovating new product lines become growth leaders in those clusters. Even though new enterprises are attracted to the clusters, innovation and product differentiation allow cluster-based enterprises to continue to be profitable and to grow. While competition improves the cluster's overall economic efficiency by weeding out inefficient enterprises, the lack of capacity to invest and innovate among competing enterprises in survival clusters—resulting from inadequate access to finance and poor managerial skills and knowledge—is still a significant bottleneck to sustainable growth for enterprises in the clusters.

In light of the increase in internal competition, the lack of differentiation within clusters is a significant underlying reason for the decline in profitability as clusters expand. A simple economic rule is that firms earn no profit in the presence of perfect competition, where firms produce homogeneous products and no restrictions are placed on entry and exit.

Profitability declines unless cluster-based entrepreneurs seek to differentiate themselves from each other by upgrading their product lines, improving production efficiency, and developing new markets. Several case studies of industrial clusters in developing countries around the world show how upgrading product lines and improving production and quality management, marketing methods, and financial methods have enabled industrial clusters to maintain profitability and grow in an environment of increasing internal competition (for example, Schmitz and Nadvi 1999; Sonobe and Otsuka 2006).

While lack of access to finance is a serious binding constraint on investment and innovation, weak managerial knowledge and skills prevent entrepreneurs based in survival clusters from developing even simple, less costly innovations to improve the efficiency of their production process and the marketability of their products. Regardless of whether or not they are located in a cluster, micro and small enterprises face difficulty in upgrading their product lines because poor access to credit keeps them from acquiring better equipment. While improving access to credit among micro and small enterprises is an important policy issue to be addressed, entrepreneurs could still improve their profitability by improving the efficiency of their existing product lines as well as the marketing of their products and services, as shown by the experience of various clusters around the world. These intrafirm reforms require managerial knowledge and skill, which entrepreneurs running micro and small enterprises in Africa generally lack.

Lack of Spatial Mobility

Another bottleneck to growth in survival-type clusters in Africa is the limited amount of opportunities for individual enterprises to improve their position by moving to an alternative location as they grow. In response to questions about constraints in the investment climate, cluster-based entrepreneurs indicated that they are especially concerned about land-related issues, such as limited availability of workspace, poor security, and weak infrastructure. Enterprises seeking to expand their production seek better locations to accommodate their growing need for space. Moving out of a survival cluster and into a better location not only provides a growth path for individual enterprises, but also an opportunity for those enterprises to form more innovation-oriented clusters. For industrial clusters to become a base for sustainable growth of the indigenous enterprise sector in Africa, development of innovation-oriented clusters is crucial.

Demand for relocation seems to be correlated with better business performance, but where can enterprises relocate, given the scarcity of alternative locations? How are the preferred locations of enterprises related to their business performance? After controlling for any specific effects from areas, industries, and individual clusters, the estimation from a simple probit model shows that enterprises with better business performance, in terms of both sales per worker and intensity of sales to nonlocal markets, are more likely to seek an alternative location (see figure 6.3). This is good news because it means that the good performers want to move. However, the inability to move to an alternative location without incurring high mobility costs constrains good performers from moving. Unlike in Nairobi—where larger industrial estates with better infrastructure are available for good performers from informal clusters (or *Jua Kali* in Kiswahili) including Kariobangi Light Industries—in most cities in Africa, no better locations are locally available for industrial activities. Thus the probability is low that productive and profitable enterprises will leave the current cluster for a better location.[1]

Figure 6.3   Marginal Effects on the Probability of Seeking an Alternative Location among Cluster-based and Outside Enterprises

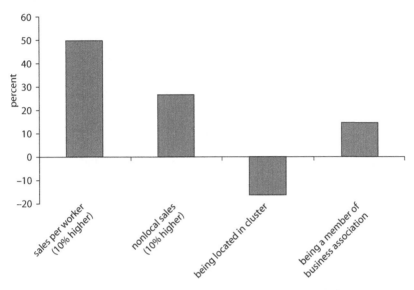

Source: Bougna and Yoshino 2009, based on the data of micro and small enterprises inside the 10 light manufacturing clusters and their outside comparators collected as part of the original five-country case studies of industrial clusters.
Note: Based on coefficient estimates on the probit model estimation of how a set of factors is related to the probability that enterprises will seek an alternative location. Only significant factors are reported.

Experiences from other regions show that urbanization facilitates the growth of industrial clusters. In their study of the location patterns of industrial clusters with multiple manufacturing sectors within three metropolitan cities in India (Chennai, Kolkata, and Mumbai), Chakravorty, Koo, and Lall (2003) find that urbanization economies drive the formation of industrial clusters rather than localization economies. The actual location of different industries depends on a complex set of factors, including accidents of history, metropolitan expansion, state regulations, especially ones that affect the land market, and industry characteristics. Single-sector industrial districts, especially those that cannot benefit from urbanization economies, are unlikely to succeed. Land use policies deeply influence industry location. A policy regime that does not allow land use to change—say, from residential to industrial use—creates significant inefficiencies in industrial location, leading to ad hoc co-location without backward and forward linkages or leap-flogging.

Successful Transformation from Informal Survival-Cluster Enterprises to Formal Enterprises

With the ability to differentiate products and spatial mobility, some survival-cluster enterprises have succeeded in transforming themselves into more formal enterprises. Sonobe, Akoten, and Otsuka (2009) analyze the profile of enterprises that used to be located in the Kariobangi Light Industries cluster in Nairobi, which is one of the 10 light manufacturing industrial clusters covered by the five-country case studies, before they relocated to formal upscale industrial areas (with direct buyer-supplier ties with multinational corporations) within Nairobi. The profile is based on their data before relocation (see table 6.1). These "graduated" enterprises had the ability to be more selective in forming backward and forward linkages with customers and input suppliers. They had the ability to reach out to customers who are more quality-conscious and to procure inputs directly from suppliers. Those are specific aspects of their overall ability to differentiate themselves from their internal competitors by taking more innovative approaches to reaching customers and developing their products. At the same time, the very fact that there was an alternative

Table 6.1   Characteristics of Graduated and Remaining Enterprises in Kariobangi Light Industries

Characteristic	Graduated enterprises	Remaining enterprises
Number of firms	7	120
Experience in formal sector (%)	71.0	62.0
Age	45.6	39.7
Years of schooling	13.0	10.9
Years of vocational training	2.6	0.9
Years of prior experience in similar business	8.7	3.9
Years of management experience	9.3	7.5
Number of employees		
1998 or 2000	17.0	4.0
2005	25.1	5.1
Marketing to quality-conscious customers (% of revenue)		
1998 or 2000	51.0	9.2
2005	55.0	6.2
Direct procurement (% of material cost)		
1998 or 2000	31.0	25.4
2005	50.7	28.8

Source: Sonobe, Akoten, and Otsuka 2009.

location within the same city was a necessary condition for their transformation from survival-level to formal enterprises.

Implications of Cluster Growth for Employment

The growth of industrial clusters has potentially positive implications for the labor market. Labor pooling is evident in the data, with cluster-based enterprises absorbing more permanent workers and outside enterprises absorbing more apprentices who are unskilled (see figure 6.4). Employment growth is another dimension of cluster growth. Industrial clusters have been a significant source of urban employment for the local labor force in Africa.

Within clusters, relatively large enterprises that can expand their markets are absorbing more workers. Even though industrial clusters are defined as concentrations of enterprises in the same or closely related industries, enterprises are heterogeneous in many respects (see figure 6.5). This implies that enterprises within the clusters are becoming more differentiated. Some

Figure 6.4   Growth in Labor Force among Cluster-based and Outside Enterprises, 2005–08

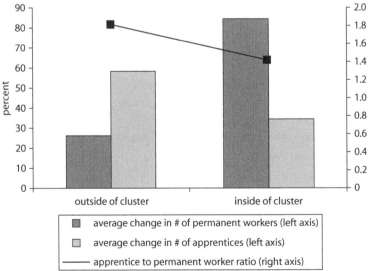

Source: Bougna and Yoshino 2009, based on the data of micro and small enterprises inside the 10 light manufacturing clusters and their outside comparators collected as part of the original five-country case studies of industrial clusters.

Figure 6.5   Growth in Employment in Cluster-based Enterprises, by Principal Sales Market, 2005–08

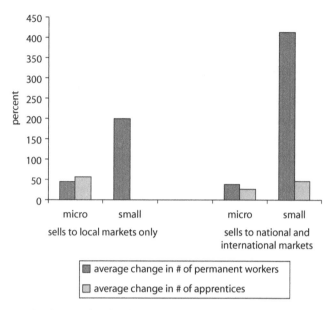

Source: Bougna and Yoshino 2009, based on the data of micro and small enterprises inside the 10 light manufacturing clusters and their outside comparators collected as part of the original five-country case studies of industrial clusters.

cluster-based enterprises are relatively large. They are able to sell their products outside of the local markets. They have grown much faster than other enterprises and employ more permanent workers. On the one hand, this underscores how better market access and growth are related. On the other hand, it indicates a possible widening of the size gap between those that participate in nonlocal markets and those that do not, as enterprises that are capable of selling their products in nonlocal markets are growing faster.

Note

1. As discussed in the next section, in Kariobangi Light Industries, a few firms have relocated from the cluster to formal industrial areas within Nairobi.

References

Bougna, Theophile, and Yutaka Yoshino. 2009. "Industrial Clusters and Micro- and Small Light Manufacturing Enterprises in Africa: Findings from Country Case Studies." Analytical background note prepared for the study.

Chakravorty, Sanjoy, Jun Koo, and Somik V. Lall. 2003. "Metropolitan Industrial Clusters: Patterns and Processes." Policy Research Working Paper 3073, World Bank, Washington, DC.

Iddrisu, Alhassan, Yukichi Mano, and Tetsushi Sonobe. 2009. "Entrepreneurial Skills and Industrial Development: The Case of a Car Repair and Metalworking Cluster in Ghana." Centre for the Study of African Economies, Department of Economics, Oxford University (February 27).

Khan, Sunday. 2009. "Industrial Clusters and Indigenous Private Sector in Africa: Cameroon Country Case Study." Background technical paper prepared for the study.

Schmitz, Hubert, and Khalid Nadvi. 1999. "Clustering and Industrialization: Introduction." *World Development* 27 (9): 1503–14.

Sonobe, Tetsushi, John E. Akoten, and Keijiro Otsuka. 2009. "The Growth Process of Informal Enterprises in Sub-Saharan Africa: A Case Study of a Metalworking Cluster in Nairobi." *Small Business Economics* [online publication], July 15.

Sonobe, Tetsushi, and Keijiro Otsuka. 2006. *Cluster-Based Industrial Development: An East Asian Model.* New York: Palgrave Macmillan.

CHAPTER 7

Building Managerial Human Capital in Africa's Survival Industrial Clusters

Enterprises in industrial clusters in Africa need to innovate if they are to overcome growth bottlenecks and move out of the survival level. Profitability declines unless cluster-based entrepreneurs seek to differentiate themselves from their competitors—both within and outside the clusters—through upgrading product lines, improving production efficiency, and developing new markets. Case studies of industrial clusters in developing countries around the world show how upgrading product lines and improving production and quality management, marketing methods, and financial methods have enabled industrial clusters to maintain profitability and grow in an environment of increasing internal competition (for example, Schmitz and Nadvi 1999; Sonobe and Otsuka 2006).

Managerial human capital, such as managers' education and their knowledge and skills in management, is a critical source of enterprises' ability to innovate and differentiate their products from those of their competitors. A series of empirical works, such as Ramachandran, Gelb, and Shah (2009), suggests that manager's education level and access to finance constitute two significant constraints on growth among indigenous African firms. These studies show that indigenous firms owned by entrepreneurs with secondary or university education achieve a higher rate of growth. A higher education level results in better managerial skills, including the ability to hire and manage larger numbers of people, to maintain accounts and records, and to access new technology. Access to education enables indigenous entrepreneurs to develop managerial skills that substitute for the information and financial networks created by nonindigenous entrepreneurs. Empirical papers on specific industrial clusters in Africa (for example, Akoten, Otsuka, and Sonobe 2006; Iddrisu, Mano, and Sonobe 2009; Sonobe, Akoten, and Otsuka 2009) also identify the lack of management and marketing knowledge among cluster-based entrepreneurs as the most serious constraint on generating spinoffs.

A small number of studies have so far explicitly estimated the impact of managerial human capital development on firm performance in a development context. While many studies have sought to relate productivity to the concept of entrepreneurship, only a few have explicitly identified the contribution of managerial skills to firms' performance. Karlan and Valdivia (2009) present a valuable piece of experiment-based evidence: a program designed to teach managerial skills to small-business entrepreneurs in Peru that improved business practices and performance. In the context of Africa, Iddrisu, Mano, and Sonobe (2009) find that entrepreneurs in a car repair and metalworking cluster in Ghana who had formal managerial training achieved better business results, on average, than those who had no formal training. There is also an increasing number of research projects evaluating the impacts of existing business development services (BDS), particularly in the context of promoting entrepreneurship by women.

Cluster-Based Pilot Managerial Skill Training Programs in Kumasi and Nairobi

Against this backdrop, the World Bank and the Foundation for Advanced Studies on International Development (FASID) implemented pilot training programs on managerial skills for cluster-based entrepreneurs. The training programs were implemented in two industrial clusters in Africa, both in the metalwork sector: one in Suame Magazine in Kumasi, Ghana, and the other in Kariobangi Light Industries in Nairobi, Kenya. These two locations were chosen because of the availability of baseline survey data conducted in 2006 by the FASID team. Boxes 7.1 and 7.2 provide a brief introduction to these two clusters.

The three-week-long training program in each location covered three basic topics: entrepreneurship, business strategy, and marketing; production management and quality assurance; and record keeping and business financial documents. A description of the format of the training is

Box 7.1

History of Suame Magazine

Located in the Suame area in Kumasi, the second largest city in Ghana and the center of the Ashanti region, Suame Magazine is possibly the largest manufacturing cluster in Africa, with approximately 10,000 enterprises and workshops in automobile repair services (garages), automobile parts production, and retail services, as well as metalworking, employing an estimated 100,000 workers. These enterprises and workshops are located in a 900,000 square meter area. The cluster originated in the 1930s when isolated craftsmen set up workshops at the site of the present Kumasi Zoo, a former army depot called Magazine during colonial times. When the workshops resettled in the current location, they kept the name. The cluster has expanded ever since in area, number of enterprises, and size of employment.

The garages are by far the largest and fastest growing sector. In developed countries, garages are scattered far and wide to serve dispersed car owners. In developing countries, most vehicles are part of business fleets. In Ghana, trailers and trucks are concentrated on the artery roads connecting major southern cities, such as Accra and port cities, with the major cities in the north, such as Tamale and Ouagadougou, the capital of Burkina Faso. Kumasi is the most important junction of these arteries. The number of vehicles on these arteries has grown continuously over the years, and the demand for garage services has increased accordingly. While garages are clustered not only in Kumasi but also in Accra and other cities, Suame Magazine is said to be larger and to have higher technical skills and better equipment than any other cluster in West Africa.

Tasks are highly specialized. Each master specializes in a particular type of service (for example, automotive electricians and engine re-borers) and in a particular type of vehicle (for example, large trucks) of a particular brand (for example, Mercedes-Benz). Collaboration among specialists is coordinated by generalist mechanics called fitters, who receive orders from car owners, determine the cause of the trouble, decide who should be involved in the repair work and how much they should be paid, and collect and distribute payments by the customers. Such coordination is actively pursued, probably because the geographic proximity among transacting parties discourages opportunistic behavior and reduces transaction costs.

Suame Magazine is equipped with a large number of machine tools, such as lathes and milling machines, and specialized machines. Skilled machinists operating these machines overhaul engines, gears, and crankshafts. Such services are

(continued next page)

Box 7.1 *(continued)*

relatively expensive and often unavailable at smaller clusters of garages. In addition to working with fitters, machinists produce simple auto parts, such as center bolts, U-bolts, and nuts, which traders buy in bulk. Machinists also repair worn gears and other parts for large firms located outside the cluster, such as lumber mills and mining companies. Moreover, they process parts for metal products, such as flour mixing machines, water pumps, and cash safes, which manufacturers fabricate using scrap metal.

The number of these machine shops has increased since the 1980s, when the Intermediate Technology Transfer Unit, a training institution established in 1980 by the Kumasi Nkrumah University of Science and Technology, assisted promising enterprises in acquiring machine tools.

While the garage sector is dominant in Suame Magazine, this concentration of garages has attracted other manufacturing activities such as blacksmiths, machinists, and parts manufacturers. Natural backward and forward linkages have formed between these enterprises and the garage sector. Manufacturers are skilled welders who could use welding machines to fabricate anything but usually specialize in specific metal products. Since they do not own machine tools, they often contract out processing work to machinists within Suame Magazine. The availability of scrap metal as a raw material within the cluster is another important source of agglomeration of multiple sectors, which are interlinked in supply chains.

Source: Iddrisu, Mano, and Sonobe 2009.

Box 7.2

History of Kariobangi Light Industries

Kariobangi Light Industries is a concentration of micro and small metalwork enterprises, as well as hardware retail shops and machinery repair service workshops, located in northeastern Nairobi (approximately 10 kilometers from Nairobi's central business district). There are approximately 300 enterprises and workshops in Kariobangi Light Industries, half of which are metalwork enterprises. The land was originally acquired in 1978 by a local member of Parliament who wished to alleviate mounting pressure for business land by jobless people in his constituency. The land was demarcated into plots and designated as a light industry area. The plots were provided to artisanal entrepreneurs who lost their employment in the formal sector as a consequence of the country's Structural Adjustment Program in the 1980s. Such informal artisanal entrepreneurs call themselves *Jua Kali*, which literally means "hot sun" in Kiswahili. The industrial area is demarcated by streets and surrounded by low-income residential areas comprising mid-rise apartment buildings and slum dwellings.

In 1982 construction of factories began, with Baraka Engineering and Kiamariga Engineering, both now closed, among the pioneers. Establishment of garages followed next. Then in 1984, Blue Rings Detergents was established. Still in operation, this is one of the factories that graduated from Kariobangi Light Industries and recently moved to Industrial Area. Around 1986 hardware shops were introduced. The service industry could not be left behind. As the population of business owners and workers grew, an entrepreneur wanted to start a hotel, but no more land was available. At that time, a slum had developed along the main road at one corner of Kariobangi Light Industries. The entrepreneur bought this land, burned down the slum, and displaced the slum dwellers. He constructed the Marphic Arc Hotel around 1986. Part of the slum was also bought by business persons who had missed the initial allocation of land.

By 1987 there was pressure to construct residential housing because of the rising population in the cluster as well as the needs of those displaced by slum demolition. This led to the building of houses on top of the factories, which occupied the ground floor. In that year, the area was connected to the electrical grid.

In the early 1990s more workers who had lost jobs in the formal sector as a result of the Structural Adjustment Program started streaming into Kariobangi Light Industries to establish enterprises or seek employment. As a result, machining factories were established, followed by scrap metal dealers and other factories. The owner of Danland Engineering was one of the beneficiaries, having acquired land following the displacement of slum dwellers.

To date, the activities that have emerged in this cluster include garages, metalwork, foundries, and retail shops. The enterprises number about 300, half of them related to metalworking. The products manufactured include foundry products (such as car spacers); lathe works, welding, and metal fabrication (steel doors, windows, furniture, cooking stoves); and mechanical machines (flour millers, feed mixers, block makers, counterweight balances, band saws, candle makers, bakery machines, and chip cutters, among others). Some companies are also beginning to produce spring and bag-weighing scales. The design for counterweight scales was copied from Avery, a British company that made these scales before closing down, while the design for spring scales was copied from a design imported from China.

Source: Akoten 2009.

provided in appendix 4. Entrepreneurs in the two clusters had very weak knowledge of basic managerial practices that are taken for granted in the formal sector. Participants were selected randomly in Suame Magazine. However, the initial attempt of randomization in Kariobangi Light Industries did not succeed because of several disruptions in the country and the city, including confusion related to the post-presidential-election violence from late 2007 to early 2008.

The ex post surveys were conducted approximately one year after the training programs were completed to evaluate the impacts of the training on business performance (growth in sales, value added, and profit) among participants and their patterns of practicing business management routines (for example, record keeping, having an organized workshop environment, advertising, and business planning).

Characteristics of Participants and Firm Performance

Basic characteristics of sample entrepreneurs in this study are shown in table 7.1. For both clusters, participants and nonparticipants had similar education levels and comparable numbers of years in business.[1] However, participants in Suame Magazine tended to have had some formal training. In Kariobangi, participants were slightly older, more likely to have worked in the formal sector, and more likely to have taken other formal technical and managerial training compared with nonparticipants.

Table 7.1   Characteristics of the Sample Entrepreneurs in Suame Magazine and Kariobangi Light Industries before Training

Characteristic	Suame Magazine		Kariobangi Light Industries	
	Participants	Nonparticipants	Participants	Nonparticipants
Number of entrepreneurs	48	80	47	72
Number of workers	6.9	5.5	3.3	4.6
Age of entrepreneurs	43.4	44.2	40.4	37.7
Years of schooling	10.3	10.1	11.5	11.2
Years of operation	12.3	13.1	8.2	8.3
Past participation in apprenticeship (%)	91.7	85.9	—	—
Past participation in formal training (%)	41.7	26.1	—	—
Formal sector experience (%)	—	—	70.2	47.2
Other formal training (%)	—	—	27.7	6.9

Sources: Mano and others 2009, 2010.
Note: — = data not collected.

With regard to firm performance prior to the training program, participants in Suame Magazine had slightly higher value added and producer surplus than nonparticipants.[2] The differences were not substantial. In contrast, participants in Kariobangi Light Industries had significantly lower value added and producer surplus than nonparticipants (see figure 7.1). The large deviation in productivity between participants and nonparticipants in Kariobangi suggests possible selection bias in participation; that is, entrepreneurs with low productivity self-selected to participate in the training. Since participation was voluntary, it was subject to the opportunity cost of entrepreneurs. Even though the training session was scheduled for late afternoon to early evening and limited to two to three hours a day, participation shortened the hours of operation for participating entrepreneurs. The time cost of participation was not negligible for busy entrepreneurs. Moreover, despite efforts to sensitize the cluster-based entrepreneurs in advance, entrepreneurs could not fully appreciate the scope of expected benefits from the program due to the post-presidential-election violence from late 2007 to early 2008, which occurred after the sensitization event was held in the cluster to inform potential participants of the planned training program.

Practice of Basic Business Routines of Participants

Based on interviews conducted during site visits to the participants' workshops, the entrepreneurs faced challenges such as poor housekeeping, lack of adequate space for their operation, lack of appropriate and suitable tools for the job, poor-quality raw materials, obsolete machine tools and equipment, poor record keeping, low sales, and limited promotional activities. Because many entrepreneurs did not keep records of business transactions, they did not keep proper track of orders they received or losses and profits they made. Since they did not clean or organize their workshop, they were often unable to find materials that were bought only a few days before, bought unnecessary materials, and faced occupational hazards. Table 7.2 and box 7.3 present some cases of actual entrepreneurs and the constraints they faced prior to the training programs.

Entrepreneurs in the two clusters had very weak knowledge of basic managerial practices that are taken for granted in the formal sector. These include bookkeeping (financial management), marketing, and efforts to improve the organization of workshops (production management). As shown in table 7.3, in Suame Magazine, prior to the training programs, less than one-third of the entrepreneurs practiced bookkeeping, advertised

Figure 7.1   Monthly Value Added and Producer Surplus before Training Programs in Suame Magazine and Kariobangi Light Industries

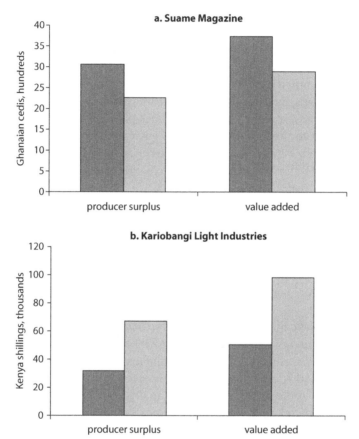

Sources: Mano and others 2009, 2010.
Note: For Suame Magazine, pretraining period is 2004 for sales revenue and value added and 2007 for business routines. Sales revenue and value added are evaluated in GHS 1,000 in 2008. For Kariobangi Light Industries, the figure compares data from 2007 and 2008.

their businesses, or had business plans based on their business records. Entrepreneurs had a better record of bookkeeping in Kariobangi Light Industries than in Suame Magazine overall. Nevertheless, only half of the Kariobangi entrepreneurs practiced bookkeeping. Less than a third in Kariobangi had ever attempted to reorganize their workshop to improve efficiency and safety.

Table 7.2   Challenges among Micro and Small Enterprises in Kariobangi Light Industries

Products produced by interviewed enterprises	Problems
Baking ovens, band saws, popcorn machines, paint mixer ovens, and a wide range of other products	· Low growth of customer base; little effort put into selling products; reduction in sales volume; poor-quality management; lack of tools
Spare parts for automobiles, gas welding rods, caliper clips, nuts, and many other metal items	Limited space for operation; poor-quality raw materials; inability to meet demand due to limited space and qualified personnel
Stainless steel catering equipment, fuel-efficient stoves and pots, and so forth	Lack of suitable equipment for work; stiff competition from former employees
Metal doors, door frames, and window frames	Unapproved location, situated on space zoned for a road; inadequate workspace; difficulty working during rainy season; inadequate tools and equipment; low sales
Casting of components for all categories of industry in ferrous and nonferrous metals	Inadequate workspace; poor lighting; lack of trust in capability of company by potential customers; perception that all products from Kariobangi are inferior
Grinding mills, office furniture, steel doors, billboards, and so forth	High cost of electricity; poor housekeeping; poor lighting
Molds for casting, dies for sheet metal blanking and forming, general services	Lack of tools and equipment; poor housekeeping; poor lighting; lack of appropriate raw materials for production
General machine shop service, provision of spare parts, building of feed mills, and so forth	Poor power supply and high cost of electricity
Nonferrous metal casting using permanent molds; products include grills, chippers, gratings, frying pans	Poor furnace design, which wastes fuel; inadequate and unsuitable space for foundry work; poor housekeeping; limited resources to meet high demand
Caliper clips for automobiles, gas welding electrodes, nuts, and so forth	Poor lighting; poor housekeeping; inadequate tools and equipment for work; inadequate workshop space; lack of educational background to register as an engineering firm
Band saws and posh mills (for grinding grain into flour)	Poor record keeping; inability to distinguish profit and cash inflow; poor cash management; frequent overdrawing of money from the business; inability to distinguish between business and personal funds; enterprise not registered despite being in operation for more than four years
Wholesale door hinges	Inability to calculate costs and prices

(continued next page)

Table 7.2   Challenges among Micro and Small Enterprises in Kariobangi Light Industries *(continued)*

Products produced by interviewed enterprises	Problems
Car part repairs; customers are private car owners and mechanics	Poor record keeping; inability to determine sales and expenses
Fabrication of all types of products	Competition from larger companies; poor cash flow; inability to raise bonds to get large contracts
Energy-saving cookers, boilers, and honey harvesting machines	Need to intensify marketing efforts; on the whole doing well; good record-keeping system and product brochures; many recommendations from customers
Door hinges	Poor record keeping; stiff competition
Candle-making machines, milking machines, and incinerators; fabrication of machines on request	Poor record-keeping system; inability to interpret information collected or to use the information for decision making; little effort made to market and sell products

Source: EDC Limited 2008.

Box 7.3

Challenges among Micro and Small Enterprises in Suame Magazine

Francis, an aluminum ingot and pan producer. Francis was a supplier of aluminum ingots. He had been in business for more than 15 years, producing an average of 500 aluminum pans a day, which he sold both locally and across the border in Mali. Francis promoted his business only through his company's trade name and logo. He employed 10 apprentices to whom he paid an allowance. His main challenge was his inability to meet demand due to limited production capacity. He had unsuccessfully searched for funding from various financial institutions to expand his capacity. His low literacy level was a challenge to his business growth, and he was looking for opportunities to develop his capacity. After gaining an understanding of his challenges, the instructors encouraged Francis to keep proper records of his finances in order to attract financiers and to keep proper records of his employees.

Dominic, a crankshaft producer. Dominic had been repairing crankshafts for more than 15 years. He estimated that there were about 20 crankshaft producers in Suame Magazine. His main challenges were "fake" bearings used in servicing crankshafts and competition from secondhand car engine dealers and other crankshaft producers. Dominic was advised to study his competitors to come up with strategies to perform better than they do. He was also encouraged to explore other markets, such as corporate bodies that have large fleets of vehicles, as opposed to relying on walk-in customers.

Peter, a producer of center bolts and U-clamps. Peter had been in business for more than 25 years, although his business had yet to be registered. He sold U-clamps and center bolts to retailers in Suame Magazine and to exporters to Lagos, Nigeria. His main challenge was pricing. He did not factor in overhead in pricing his products. His prices were not fixed and varied depending on the quantity being sold and the customer's bargaining power. He also sold on credit, which sometimes affected his working capital. Peter was coached on how to include overhead costs in his costing and pricing. He was also advised to keep good records of his stock.

Muntari, a producer of commercial gas cookers. Muntari had been in business for more than 15 years. He had 18 apprentices. His main challenges were his inability to get an agent to distribute his products and his lack of a showroom. His financial controls were weak, which had resulted in losses from fraud. Muntari served as the chief engineer, general manager, human resource manager, and bookkeeper in the enterprise, thus limiting the time he could devote to marketing his products and generating new sales. Muntari was advised to consider hiring a salesperson to increase his marketing capacity. He was also advised to hire an assistant to assume some of his responsibilities.

Kwaku, a producer of money safes. Kwaku produced both money safes and strong-room steel doors, mainly for banks and other financial institutions. Kwaku's biggest challenge was finding funding sources to expand his business. He was advised to maintain proper records and to develop a business plan.

Ahmed, a lining cylinder producer. Ahmed was in partnership with his elder brother. He was involved in day-to-day running of the business and remitted a share of profits to his brother, who had provided the capital used to aquire the machines. Ahmed's main challenge was his inability to raise capital to replace his obsolete machines. He was advised to develop a business plan, open an account, and save money toward replacing the old machinery.

Source: EDC Limited 2007.

Table 7.3   Practice of Business Routines in Suame Magazine and Kariobangi Light Industries before Training

	Suame Magazine		Kariobangi Light Industries	
Routine	Participants	Nonparticipants	Participants	Nonparticipants
Record keeping	18.8	27.0	46.8	61.6
Advertise own business	29.2	30.3	—	—
Brand own products	—	—	29.2	33.3
Have plan based on business records	14.6	19.1	—	—
Improving workshop organization	—	—	31.9	29.2

Sources: Mano and others 2009, 2010.
Note: — = data not collected.

As shown in table 7.3, except for financial management (record keeping), there was no significant difference between the business routines of participants and nonparticipants before the training programs were conducted. Marketing-related routines, such as advertising their business or branding their products, had very similar rates of practice between the two groups. The same was true for business planning routines (whether an enterprise had a business plan based on business records) as well as production management routines (whether an enterprise had ever reorganized the workshop to improve work efficiency and safety). For record keeping, in both Suame Magazine and Kariobangi Light Industries, participants had lower rates of practice than nonparticipants before the training.

In the area of financial management, participants generally believed that their business was too small to keep records and that record-keeping practice was only for large-scale, profitable enterprises. They saw record keeping as laborious and time-consuming. All of those visited had official receipt books but issued receipts only when requested by the customer. When they ran out of receipts, they used those of their neighbors. They were cautioned by the trainers of the training program that the practice could land them in serious trouble, especially if they gave out receipts for payments they had not collected from the customer. All the participants kept their own business records, keeping source documents in all sorts of places such as old cocoa sacks, paper cartons, and loosely hanging winter jackets. The inappropriateness of such practices was discussed during the visits and later in class.

Assessing the Impacts of Training Programs

Follow-up surveys were conducted approximately one year after the training programs were given in both clusters in order to collect data on changes in business performance and practices among training participants and nonparticipants relative to the baseline survey data collected prior to the training. The impacts of the training programs are assessed both in gross as well as in net, separating out factors other than the training programs that may have contributed to the changes.

Gross Impacts

The training programs had a visible, immediate impact on the ground. Evidence suggests that the participants' business routines changed immediately after the training, and their business performance improved. Formal impact evaluation in the form of ex post surveys was conducted in the two clusters approximately one year after the pilot training programs. The survey in Suame Magazine covered all participants (48) as well as nonparticipants (80). The survey in Kariobangi Light Industries could not cover all participants. Out of 55 participants, eight refused to cooperate, had closed down, could not be reached, or had relocated outside the cluster. Thus the survey covered the remaining 47 participants as well as 72 nonparticipants.

In a comparison of two key indicators of business performance—value added and gross profit—before and after the training programs, participants (treatment group) recorded higher rates of growth in business performance after the training than nonparticipants (control group; see figure 7.2).[3] In Kariobangi Light Industries, the difference between participants and nonparticipants is very clear. In the case of Suame Magazine, the difference between participants and nonparticipants is very clear only among manufacturers. The manufacturers who participated in the training recorded positive growth in value added as well as in gross profit, while nonparticipating manufacturers experienced negative growth in both. Both participants and nonparticipants among machinists experienced a reduction in value added and gross profit in the period after the training, with participating machinists experiencing only slightly smaller declines than nonparticipating machinists. The majority of machinists in Suame Magazine run their operations using machinery and workspace they rent from the owners. The fact that there were only a few owners among participants may explain the weak gross impacts of the training among machinists in contrast to the visible impacts among manufacturers.

With regard to business routines, those who participated in the training programs showed a stronger tendency to adopt new business routines in financial management (bookkeeping), production management (organization of workshops), and marketing (see figure 7.3). In Suame Magazine, the adoption of business routines was equally visible among machinists and manufacturers who participated in the training.

Figure 7.2   Growth in Value Added and Gross Profit before and after the Training Programs

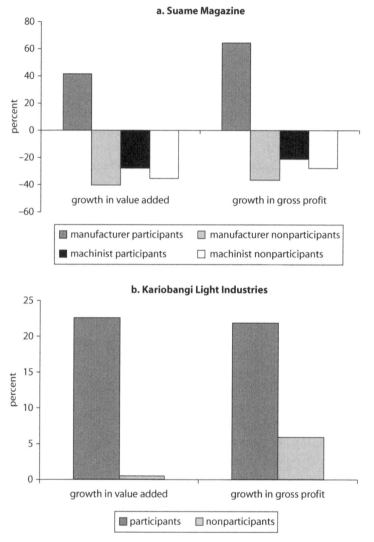

Sources: Mano and others 2009, 2010.

Net Impacts

In order to estimate the net impacts of the training programs on business performance and business routines among entrepreneurs in the two clusters, econometric analysis is conducted using the differences-in-differences (DID) approach, while controlling for other factors that influence business performance and practices.

Figure 7.3   Rate of Practicing Business Routines before and after the Training Programs

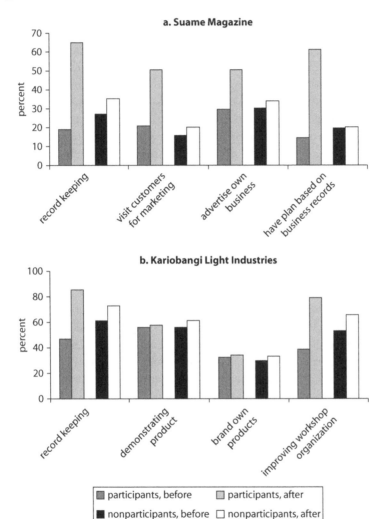

Sources: Mano and others 2009, 2010.

Suame Magazine. In Suame Magazine, not all entrepreneurs initially participating completed the three-week program. Both the treatment-received analysis (comparing participants and nonparticipants) and the intention-to-treat analysis (comparing the initial participants, including those who dropped out, and those who did not participate from the outset) were employed to deal with the discrepancy between the assigned treatment and the actual training received.

In Suame Magazine, participation in training had a positive net impact on business performance among manufacturers. Table 7.4 presents the results of the DID regression using random-effect and fixed-effect models for the treatment-received analysis. Since full participation (not dropping out during the program) might depend on their business performance, instrumental variable (IV) analysis was used to address the endogeneity problem. *Participant* is a dummy variable to indicate whether the entrepreneur was a participant or not. This variable controls for the baseline difference between the treatment group (participants) and the control group (nonparticipants). The interaction term among the *participant* variable, the *year* dummy for 2008, which captures the period after training, and the *manufacturer* dummy measures the net impact of training among manufacturers. Similarly, the interaction term among *participant, year 2008*, and *machinist* measures the net impact of training among machinists. Other control variables are the entrepreneur's characteristics, including age, whether local (from Ashanti) or not, years of schooling, experience of apprentice training, past participation in formal training, years of enterprise operation, and whether the entrepreneur is a machinist or not. The net impacts of the training program on sale revenue, value added, and gross profit were equivalent to GHS 25,000, GHS 18,000, and GHS 15,000, respectively. These numbers are equivalent to 91, 145, and 160 percent, respectively, of the average pre-training sales revenue, value added, and gross profit levels of the participating manufacturers. The estimated impact of training on the machinists' business performance was insignificant. Among entrepreneur characteristics, the more educated entrepreneurs tended to attain greater value added and gross profit.

Participation in training had a positive net impact on business routine practices among both manufacturers and machinists. The specification of the DID regression functions is the same for both business routines and business performance (see table 7.5). The estimated net impact of training suggests that, among manufacturers, 22 percent of the participants started visiting customers for marketing purposes, 59 percent started keeping records, and 48 percent started analyzing records as a result of the training. Among machinists, 27 percent of the participants started visiting customers for marketing purposes, 18 percent started keeping records, and 29 percent started analyzing records. Among other characteristics, educated entrepreneurs tended to keep business records and make business plans on the basis of those records.

Table 7.4 **Impact of the Managerial Skill Training on Business Performance in Suame Magazine: Difference-in-Difference Random-Effect and Fixed-Effect Models (Treatment-Received Analysis)**

Dependent variable	Sales revenue	Value added	Gross profit	Visiting customers	Keeping records	Analyzing records
a: Random-effect IV model						
Participant × manufacturer × year 2008	25.34**	18.05**	15.05**	0.222**	0.593***	0.481***
	(2.09)	(2.16)	(1.99)	(2.26)	(4.56)	(3.42)
Participant × machinist × year 2008	−6.008	7.145	2.629	0.270**	0.183**	0.292***
	(−0.18)	(0.33)	(0.14)	(2.40)	(2.29)	(3.32)
Participant × manufacturer	−13.25	−9.932	−5.931	0.107*	−0.045	−0.041
	(−1.08)	(−1.31)	(−0.81)	(0.88)	(−0.39)	(−0.36)
Participant × machinist	32.84	10.95	14.36	0.094	0.101	0.142*
	(0.92)	(0.59)	(1.13)	(0.81)	(0.86)	(1.12)
Age	−0.531	−0.284	−0.181	−0.003	0.003	0.004
	(−0.88)	(−0.77)	(−0.69)	(−0.92)	(0.59)	(0.92)
From Ashanti	0.028	4.950	3.657	−0.039	0.074	0.079
	(0.00)	(0.54)	(0.37)	(−0.44)	(0.77)	(0.86)
Years of schooling	3.218**	2.041**	1.592**	0.008	0.037**	0.022
	(2.15)	(2.18)	(2.15)	(0.81)	(1.96)	(1.10)
Apprentice training	19.49	6.190	3.234	0.066	−0.052	−0.112
	(1.38)	(0.46)	(0.27)	(0.50)	(−0.30)	(−0.75)
Years of operation	0.212	0.147	−0.014	−0.002	−0.001	0.003
	(0.47)	(0.43)	(−0.06)	(−0.54)	(−0.30)	(0.89)
Machinist	61.46**	51.21***	39.75***	0.094	0.116	0.060
	(3.22)	(3.57)	(4.19)	(1.13)	(1.34)	(1.18)

(continued next page)

Table 7.4 Impact of the Managerial Skill Training on Business Performance in Suame Magazine: Difference-in-Difference Random-Effect and Fixed-Effect Models (Treatment-Received Analysis) *(continued)*

Dependent variable	Sales revenue	Value added	Gross profit	Visiting customers	Keeping records	Analyzing records
b: Fixed-effect IV model						
Participant × manufacturer × year 2008	25.34*	18.05**	15.05**	0.222**	0.593***	0.482***
	(1.76)	(2.16)	(1.99)	(2.01)	(4.49)	(4.68)
Participant × machinist × year 2008	−7.054	6.42	1.974	0.268***	0.182**	0.290***
	(−0.25)	(0.30)	(0.10)	(2.93)	(2.43)	(3.21)
Hausman test χ² (*p* value)	†	0.42	0.35	†	5.69	1.12
		(1.000)	(1.000)		(0.682)	(0.997)

Source: Mano and others 2010.

Note: The number of observations is 429. Panel a reports all the estimates of the coefficients of the random-effect model. The interactions between the dummy for machinist and the year dummies (2002, 2004, and 2008) are included in the estimation, but are not reported. Panel b highlights the DID estimate of the treatment effect. *t*-statistics based on robust standard errors are in parentheses.

*** *p* < 0.01.
** *p* < 0.05.
* *p* < 0.10.
† Model fitted on the data fails to meet the asymptotic assumptions of the Hausman specification test.

Table 7.5   Impact of Managerial Skill Training on Business Performance and Business Routines in Kariobangi Light Industries: Average Treatment of Treated Estimation by DID-Matching Estimator

Dependent variable	DID-PSM estimates of training effect
Sales revenue	53.10*
	(1.90)
Value added	59.83*
	(1.93)
Gross profit	57.83*
	(1.86)
Keeping records	0.182**
	(2.26)
Analyzing records	0.182**
	(2.40)
Organized work space	0.301***
	(4.09)

Source: Mano and others 2009.
Note: The local linear regression matching method developed by Heckman, Ichimura, and Todd (1997, 1998) was used to match participants and nonparticipants. Sales revenue, value added, and gross profit are measured in K Sh 1,000 per month between June and November. The DID-PSM is based on the local linear matching. Standard errors are in parentheses.
*** $p < 0.01$.
** $p < 0.05$.
* $p < 0.10$.

Kariobangi Light Industries. In Kariobangi Light Industries, where randomization was not successful, the simple DID approach suffers from selection bias.[4] In general, the DID-matching method performs better to the extent that the ability to grow is correlated with the observed characteristics of the entrepreneur or the enterprise.[5] DID-matching estimators can eliminate the effect of time-invariant characteristics on outcome, thus reducing the selection bias. The estimator matches each participant with other sample entrepreneurs whose covariates are similar, but who did not participate in the training.

Table 7.5 presents the results of estimated average treatment of treated using the DID-matching estimator (see appendix 5 for details). We employ the DID propensity score matching (PSM) estimator.[6] The training program had positive impacts on business performance among participants in Kariobangi Light Industries. The impact of the training on sales revenue, value added, and gross profit are K Sh 53,000, K Sh 60,000, and K Sh 58,000, respectively, which are all statistically significant. These are equivalent to 44, 118, and 164 percent, respectively, of the average pretraining sales revenue, value added, and gross profit levels of the participating manufacturers.

The training program had positive impacts on management behavior among participants because it got them to introduce formal management techniques. In Kariobangi Light Industries, the training increased the probability that participants made improvements in their bookkeeping and workspace organization a part of their routine by 18 and 30 percent, respectively.

Do improvements in business routines improve business performance? In the current data, it is not feasible to perform a dynamic analysis of how improvements in business routines, such as record keeping or better organization of workshops, lead to growth in value added or profitability. However, as long as we analyze the cross-sectional data, there is a correlation between business routines and business performance. Table 7.6 presents the results of ordinary least squares (OLS) regressions on value added and producer surplus based on the cross-section data in Kariobangi Light Industries. In this exercise, we use data on the pretraining situation and do not distinguish between participants and nonparticipants. It turns out that those entrepreneurs who kept records had greater value added and producer surplus at their workshops than did the other entrepreneurs, by 50 and 76 percent, respectively.[7] Improvements in workshop organization have positive coefficients, as expected, but the association with business performance is not statistically significant.

Implications of the Results

The results of the initial impact evaluation of the pilot training program conducted in the two clusters overall support the hypothesis that upgrading managerial knowledge and skills among cluster-based entrepreneurs leads to improvements in their business performance and business routines. Participation in the experimental managerial training program was associated with larger growth in sales revenue, value added, and gross profit. In both locations, participation in the training program more than doubled the value added and gross profit of participants in *net* terms. Participation in the training program was also associated with improvements in managerial practices, such as record keeping, active marketing, and workshop reorganization to improve the physical efficiency in production.

The importance of managerial skill development among micro and small enterprises is increasingly recognized by development partners. The World Bank Group's Joint International Development Association (IDA) and International Finance Corporation (IFC) Micro, Small and Medium

Table 7.6   OLS Model Estimates of Pretraining Value Added and Gross Profit

Variable	In value added	In gross profit
Record keeping	0.415**	0.568**
	(0.205)	(0.245)
Improving workshop organization	0.123	0.089
	(0.204)	(0.265)
Entrepreneurs' age	0.004	0.003
	(0.012)	(0.013)
Years of schooling	0.063**	0.022
	(0.029)	(0.029)
Formal sector experience	0.167	0.184
	(0.187)	(0.235)
Other formal training	−0.299	−0.363
	(0.238)	(0.295)
Years of operation	0.029**	0.040**
	(0.014)	(0.017)
Intercept	2.308***	2.162***
	(0.575)	(0.640)
Number of observations	115	107
Adjusted R^2	0.100	0.053

Source: Mano and others 2009.
Note: The table reports 2007 data. The value added and producer surplus are monthly averages between June and November. Robust standard errors are in parentheses.
*** $p < 0.01$.
** $p < 0.05$.
* $p < 0.10$.

Enterprise Pilot Program for Africa, which has provided technical assistance in eight countries for the approved amount of US$354 million to date, has a component covering BDS and entrepreneurship development.[8] Results from this program component are measurable in terms of capacity building and sustainability of the overall supply of BDS in the market as well as improved productivity and job creation among micro, small, and medium enterprises as a result of improved BDS. In fact, the impact evaluation conducted under the joint IDA-IFC program corroborates the findings on the effectiveness of managerial training from the pilot training programs in the two clusters. In 2009 the Japan International Cooperation Agency launched a development study on quality and productivity improvement for the *kaizen* project in Ethiopia (*kaizen* means continuous improvement in Japanese). The project focuses on eliminating waste, improving productivity, and achieving sustained, continual improvement in production and marketing activities of individual companies. This effort is expected to result in a set of policies that promote improved management and productivity of small and medium enterprises in Ethiopia.

The uniqueness of the findings from the pilot training programs is a result of drawing on the positive impacts of targeted managerial skills training in two geographically focused industrial clusters for entrepreneurs managing micro and informal enterprises with very limited business literacy. Most other programs are intended for formal enterprises and cover a broad geographic area.[9]

A simple comparison of costs and benefits from the Kariobangi Light Industries cluster suggests a potentially high economic return from managerial skills training targeted to entrepreneurs operating micro and small enterprises in industrial clusters in Africa.[10] The potential benefits are even larger once we take into account likely positive externalities from knowledge spillovers from participants to nonparticipants within clusters. While value chain–based vertical clusters or virtually connected industry associations could also encourage such spillovers, geographically based industrial clusters might facilitate such knowledge spillover more easily and quickly because of the physical proximity of entrepreneurs. The basic level of knowledge and skills might be easier to replicate by observing and imitating neighbors' products and practices.[11]

While this finding may provide a basis for justifying a public policy to provide managerial skills training to entrepreneurs in the context of private sector development in Africa, the sustainability of such a public policy needs to be addressed. In the long run, managerial skills training can be provided on a market basis through private BDS providers, rather than through grants as a result of public policies. If the return on managerial training is high at the firm level, entrepreneurs individually or collectively should want to invest in training opportunities. One reason why they do not is the presence of search costs for entrepreneurs acting individually. The search costs for individual entrepreneurs could be lowered if they would act collectively within clusters. But there is a coordination failure in collectively seeking training opportunities. Even though industrial clusters solve the "hold-up" problem in building buyer-supplier relations (see chapter 3), investment in collective training might still suffer from the free-rider problem. Is the joint action aspect of industrial clusters sufficient to avoid such coordination failures? In order to develop sustainable markets for BDS and more clearly define the benefits of public policy intervention in managerial training, further inquiries on both the demand and the supply sides of BDS in the context of industrial clusters are necessary.

Notes

1. Entrepreneurs in the two clusters were predominantly male. In Suame Magazine, they were almost exclusively male. This is consistent with the findings from the ongoing regional study of the World Bank on gender and entrepreneurship, which has found strong industry sorting vis-à-vis gender of entrepreneurs. Women entrepreneurs are highly concentrated in textiles and apparel as well as food, but rare in other industries.

2. Producer surplus is sales revenue minus variable costs, which are measured as the sum of the costs of materials, labor, subcontracting, and electricity.

3. In Suame Magazine, the impact evaluation was conducted by comparing participants and nonparticipants (treatment-received analysis) as well as by comparing the initial participants, including those who dropped out, and those who did not participate from the outset (intention-to-treat analysis).

4. DID provides unbiased estimates of training impact on, say, value added, if the outcomes for participants and nonparticipants do not differ in the ability to increase value added, in a hypothetical case. If participants tend to have not just smaller businesses but also less ability to expand them than nonparticipants in the absence of the training, the DID method fails to eliminate the selection bias.

5. Heckman, Ichimura, and Todd (1997, 1998) and Smith and Todd (2005) find that DID-matching estimators perform better than cross-section-matching estimators.

6. DID's PSM estimator is based on local linear matching proposed by Heckman, Ichimura, and Todd (1997, 1998). Following Heckman, Ichimura, and Todd (1997), we reduce potential bias as much as possible by matching participants with nonparticipants operating the same type of manufacturing business in the same geographic area and by using data from the post-training survey in which the same questionnaire was used for participants and nonparticipants. The covariates used for matching are time-invariant or come from the pretraining period, that is, years of operation, age, years of schooling, working experience in the formal sector, and participation in past formal training.

7. These numbers are obtained by converting the estimated coefficients of record keeping in the first and second columns as follows: $\exp(0.415) = 1.51$ and $\exp(0.568) = 1.76$.

8. The seven countries in the pilot program are Ghana, Kenya, Madagascar, Mali, Nigeria, Tanzania, and Uganda. The first assistance projects were approved in December 2003.

9. The IDA competitiveness projects, like the one in Kenya, do, in some cases, include components of capacity-building micro enterprises in the informal sector. Assistance is provided through matching-grant schemes.

10. The results from the impact evaluation of the program in Kariobangi Light Industries, for example, suggest that the net effect of the training program on participants was an increase in profit of K Sh 45,000 a month each on average, which is equivalent to US$600 a month. With all 47 participants, this meant US$28,200 additional profit a month or US$338,400 a year. This is more than three times higher than the total cost of the training program in Kariobangi, including the opportunity cost for participants in terms of forgone profit during the three weeks of training.

11. Although not econometrically tested, there are signs of knowledge spillover from participants to nonparticipants regarding management techniques. Not only participants but also nonparticipants started adopting new business routines, such as record keeping, over the same period.

References

Akoten, John. 2009. "Industrial Clusters and Indigenous Private Sector in Africa: The Case of Kenya." Background technical paper prepared for the study.

Akoten, John, Keijiro Otsuka, and Tetsushi Sonobe. 2006. "The Development of the Footwear Industry in Ethiopia: How Different Is It from the East Asian Experience?" FASID Discussion Paper, FASID, Tokyo.

EDC Limited. 2007. "Training Report: Implementation of Pilot Cluster Business Management Training Programs in Ghana (Kumasi)." Consultancy report, World Bank, Washington, DC.

————. 2008. "Training Report: Implementation of Pilot Cluster Business Management Training Programs in Kenya (Nairobi)." Consultancy report, World Bank, Washington, DC.

Heckman, James J., Hidehiko Ichimura, and Petra Todd. 1997. "Matching as an Econometric Evaluation Estimator: Evidence from Evaluating a Job Training Programme." *Review of Economic Studies* 64 (4): 605–54.

————. 1998. "Matching as an Econometric Evaluation Estimator." *Review of Economic Studies* 65 (2): 261–94.

Iddrisu, Alhassan, Yukichi Mano, and Tetsushi Sonobe. 2009. "Entrepreneurial Skills and Industrial Development: The Case of a Car Repair and Metalworking Cluster in Ghana." Centre for the Study of African Economies, Department of Economics, Oxford University (February 27).

Karlan, Dean, and Martin Valdivia. 2009. "Teaching Entrepreneurship: Impact of Business Training on Microfinance Clients and Institutions." Working Paper 107, Yale University, New Haven, CT.

Mano, Yukichi, John Akoten, Keijiro Otsuka, and Tetsushi Sonobe. 2009. "Impacts of Managerial Training: The Case of a Metalworking Cluster in Nairobi." Background technical paper prepared for the study.

Mano, Yukichi, Alhassan Iddrisu, Yutaka Yoshino, and Tetsushi Sonobe. 2010. "An Impact Evaluation of Managerial Training in Sub-Saharan Africa: A Case Study of a Metalworking Cluster in Kumasi." Background technical paper prepared for the study.

Ramachandran, Vijaya, Alan Gelb, and Manju Shah. 2009. *Africa's Private Sector: What's Wrong with the Business Environment and What to Do about It.* Washington, DC: Center for Global Development.

Schmitz, Hubert, and Khalid Nadvi. 1999. "Clustering and Industrialization: Introduction." *World Development* 27 (9): 1503–14.

Smith, J. A., and Petra Todd. 2005. "Does Matching Overcome LaLonde's Critique of Nonexperimental Estimators?" *Journal of Econometrics* 125 (1-2): 305–53.

Sonobe, Tetsushi, John E. Akoten, and Keijiro Otsuka. 2009. "The Growth Process of Informal Enterprises in Sub-Saharan Africa: A Case Study of a Metalworking Cluster in Nairobi." *Small Business Economics* [online publication], July 15.

Sonobe, Tetsushi, and Keijiro Otsuka. 2006. *Cluster-Based Industrial Development: An East Asian Model.* New York: Palgrave Macmillan.

CHAPTER 8

Policy Implications: Turning Survival into Growth

Raising survival-level industrial clusters to a more dynamic, innovating state is an important avenue for fostering the growth of micro and small enterprises and building a more viable domestic private sector in Africa. Spontaneously formed industrial clusters have the potential to be natural incubators for micro and small enterprises. However, their low capacity for innovation has kept them at the subsistence level so far.

The constraints will stifle their growth unless national efforts are undertaken to improve the business environment and the investment climate. An improved business environment is a precondition for more middle-size enterprises to emerge in the private sector, a group that is currently missing in Africa. An improved investment climate at the national level would include improved access to finance, establishment of proper market institutions and infrastructure, and reduction of the transaction costs of doing business by removing administrative barriers and inefficient regulations.

These general improvements, however, need to be complemented by more specific policies relevant to survival-type natural industrial clusters in Africa and the micro and small enterprises within them. In discussing the policy implications of the empirical findings presented in the preceding chapters, this chapter highlights three core policy areas that are directly relevant to fostering the growth of survival-type clusters. These three areas are building managerial skills, instituting sound spatial and urbanization policies, and supporting market expansion through regional integration. This chapter also discusses the implications of cluster development policies undertaken by some African countries.

Building Managerial Skills

Key elements that will help micro and small enterprises to build linkages with external markets are managerial education, skill development, and improved access to credit. Managerial skill training in African clusters is one small but important step toward developing the strong indigenous private sector observed in other regions of the world. Cluster-based managerial skill development is relevant to developing countries in three ways.

Cluster-based managerial training has immediate potential for knowledge spillover within clusters. While value chain–based vertical clusters or virtually connected industry associations could also encourage such spillover, geographically based industrial clusters have the potential to facilitate such knowledge spillover easily and quickly because physical proximity allows entrepreneurs to observe and imitate neighbors' products and practices.

Maintaining profitability in industrial clusters, facilitated by upgrading the managerial skills of entrepreneurs, can have a positive impact on youth employment. While managerial skills development is a general concern at the national level, micro and small enterprises in industrial clusters are perhaps more acutely constrained by the lack of such skills than are other firms. Industrial clusters continuously attract new workers, particularly young, inexperienced apprentices eager to earn more income. Clusters often are immediate sources of employment and skills acquisition for Africa's growing young labor force. In Africa, like elsewhere in the world, apprentices learn basic production techniques from their masters. However, unlike apprentices in developed countries, they do not have opportunities to learn management skills, in large part because their masters have little knowledge of such techniques themselves.

Managerial skill development among cluster-based entrepreneurs may not be the only positive story resulting from cluster growth, but it could provide a springboard for transforming informal enterprises. Beyond the growth of industrial clusters, enhancement of managerial skills would foster formalization of informal micro enterprises. Enterprises that have recently relocated from Kariobangi to formal upscale industrial areas within Nairobi, which have direct buyer-supplier ties with multinational corporations, tend to have owners who have more previous work experience in the formal sector; they are older, better schooled, and more experienced as managers. They are also more capable of selling their products to quality-conscious customers. These graduates have the ability to be more selective in forming backward and forward linkages with customers and input suppliers.

A simple cost-benefit analysis of the training program in Kariobangi Light Industries shows that targeting such training at cluster-based micro and small enterprises could potentially have a high economic return. While this may justify the role of public policy in providing cluster-targeted managerial skill training, market-based provision of such training is equally important. In the long run, managerial skill training should be provided on a market basis through private providers of business development services (BDS) rather than through grants responding to public policies. BDS are nonfinancial services and products offered to entrepreneurs at various stages of their business. These services are aimed primarily at transferring skills or business advice. In order to develop sustainable markets for BDS and define more clearly the benefit of public policy intervention in managerial training, it is important to gain a better understanding of the demand for BDS in the context of industrial clusters. The findings from the pilot training programs reported here suggest that cluster-targeted managerial skill development programs are effective, at least in the short to medium term.

Sound Spatial and Urbanization Policy

Two of the most serious constraints on the investment climate in Africa are weak access to land and lack of a sound policy framework to support market-oriented allocation of land. Providing an incentive for enterprises to choose an optimal location and reducing the costs of mobility are crucial factors that will enable this formalization process.

An incentive framework for firm mobility includes improved availability of alternative locations. "Graduates" in the informal cluster in Nairobi are supported partly by the availability of alternative locations suitable for micro and small enterprises as they grow. Sound spatial planning and land use policy, particularly at the local level, in the context of urban planning is important in this regard. This includes optimal spatial allocation of infrastructure and other public goods, transparent and predictable zoning policy, and efforts to address negative externalities from agglomeration such as congestion and pollution.

Predictability in zoning policies is critical for the growth of micro and small enterprises. In a few cases, government, at either the national or local level, has initiated a policy to relocate manufacturing enterprises to ease urban congestion. While creating more space, such a policy also undermines the firms' existing forward and backward linkages because the new location is farther from the firms' suppliers and customers. Some key externalities from agglomeration also seem to have been lost, such as knowledge spillover and local economies of scale through subcontracting that benefited these firms in their old location. Relocating firms from a congested area to a more spacious area could attract new entrants who may have been deterred from entering previously because of congestion and lack of access to land in the existing agglomerations. Even though these relocations incur adjustment costs for the incumbent firms, they may provide growth to the sector itself in the long run if sufficient agglomeration occurs at the new location. For that to happen, the government's zoning policy has to be predictable. Frequent shifts in zoning requirements could deter new entries and new investments because of the possibility that these entrants and investors might not be able to recover their sunk costs.

As discussed in chapter 6, experiences in countries such as China, India, and Japan present a clear case that, for growth of industrial clusters to be sustainable, localization economies from clustering need to be matched with urbanization economies. The level of urbanization is lower in African cities than in major metropolises in Asian countries. However, in large cities like Nairobi, urbanizing economies at the city level do exist, together with localization economies within a single industrial cluster. In Nairobi a few owners in informal clusters (or *Jua Kali* in Kiswahili) are former employees of formal large enterprises. This is a result of urbanization economies rather than localization economies. There are virtually no direct buyer-supplier linkages or subcontracting between large enterprises in industrial zones and micro enterprises in spontaneously formed agglomerations. These two types of firms are not even co-located. However, they are indirectly linked through labor mobility and firm mobility based on urbanization economies.

Flexibility in land use and building regulations is the key if enterprises are to choose an optimal location and benefit from co-location and co-clustering. More generally, it is important to have spatially blind institutions to facilitate economic density. The necessary institutions governing land markets include a comprehensive land registry, credible mechanisms for contract enforcement and conflict resolution, flexible zoning laws, and versatile subdivision regulations that help rather than hinder the conversion of land for different uses (World Bank 2009b). Flexibility in zoning policies does not mean an absence of policy. In fact, urban planning in Africa is generally weak and often nonexistent. The absence of formal structures allows agglomeration of footloose enterprises, such as one-person enterprises, particularly in less capital-intensive sectors such as services, to emerge quite naturally. In such cases, entrepreneurs do choose optimal locations. However, lack of a formal policy framework leads the government to take ad hoc or informal measures in an effort to ease congestion.

Spatially corrective infrastructure to reduce distance (for example, new roads) and create density is important for urbanization because it unifies labor markets and facilitates labor mobility. However, this should be complemented by development of spatially blind institutions such as a land registration system. Successful urbanization has shown that fluid land markets and empowered local governments often precede investment in such infrastructure (World Bank 2009b).

Supporting Market Expansion through Regional Integration

Penetration into global markets outside of Africa continues to be a big challenge for micro and small enterprises in Africa. However, deeper regional economic integration and improved cross-border trade facilitation at the regional level provide a more immediate avenue for domestic entrepreneurs to form links with external markets. Policies can also provide an environment in which cluster-based micro and small enterprises can be better linked with larger enterprises that have access to global markets, including foreign-owned enterprises.

Regional exports are low-hanging fruits even for those enterprises. As noted by Sonobe and Otsuka (2006) for Asian clusters and by Akoten and Otsuka (2007) and Oyelaran-Oyeyinka and McCormick (2007) for African clusters, trader-manufacturer networks play a pivotal role in linking cluster-based products and nonlocal markets, including cross-border regional markets. Sonobe and Otsuka (2006) note that some cluster-based innovation is driven by merchants and traders (as opposed to producers and engineers).

Regional integration and improved efficiency in cross-border trade provides an immediate channel for external market linkages through which micro and small entrepreneurs can improve their access to formal trade channels. The domestic investment climate is important for regional integration. Firm-level data show that, while foreign ownership is a factor driving the intensity of global exports, regional exports, where African domestic enterprises are more active, are relatively more sensitive to behind-the-border domestic constraints such as inferior power services and customs delays (Yoshino 2008). Reducing behind-the-border domestic constraints encourages more regional manufacturing trade.

Deepened regional integration provides opportunities for micro and small enterprises to expand their market space. Data from the five-country case studies suggest that, for micro and small light manufacturers, the vast majority of export destinations are neighboring countries such as the Central African Republic, Chad, Equatorial Guinea, Gabon, and Nigeria for Cameroonian enterprises; Burkina Faso, Côte d'Ivoire, Mali, Niger, Nigeria, and Togo for Ghanaian enterprises; and the Democratic Republic of Congo, Rwanda, Somalia, Sudan, Tanzania, and Uganda for Kenyan enterprises. Not only light manufacturing but also service providers export regionally. For example, information technology enterprises in Rwanda provide services to Burundi and the Democratic Republic of Congo. Data show that micro and small enterprises that sell in those markets tend to have grown more in the past three years than those that do not.

Thus regional trade facilitation can enhance the ability of micro and small enterprises to broaden their market opportunities. In many countries, particularly landlocked countries, cross-border trade with neighboring countries is often conducted informally, without being recorded in the official customs data. The costs of trading in the formal sector must be reduced by allowing better access to market information, better access to trade finance and insurance, better cross-border infrastructure including roads and storage facilities, and more efficient transactions through customs. Improvements in these areas would encourage participation in formal trade as opposed to informal transactions.

Trade in services is another area where opportunities exist to expand regional trade. Growth of trade in services has a spillover effect on trade in goods by reducing various costs related to trading. For example, a framework for trade in financial services will not only support the expansion of exports from those countries with more advanced financial services sectors, but also improve access to finance and insurance as well as support the expansion of exports of goods and services from countries and regions within countries that have limited access to such services. Similarly, a reduction in barriers to cross-border provision of transport services could lead to important economies of scale and improved access to higher-quality and cheaper transport services for exporters of goods. Regional trade in BDS will provide more opportunities for micro and small enterprises to acquire technical management skills.

Government Cluster Development Policies

Building a strong domestic private sector is a policy priority around the world. Many countries in the past took protectionist measures to promote infant domestic industries and discourage imports, a policy proven to be unsuccessful in the long run. Today, some African national governments are interested in using clusters as a tool for raising the international competitiveness of domestic industries. In developing cluster strategies, it is important for governments to leverage the natural dynamics of agglomeration in spontaneously formed clusters as a means to integrate these clusters in the formal economy. A few governments recognize the synergy between policies to support micro, small, and medium enterprises and strategies to develop clusters (see boxes 8.1–8.4). However, the notion of clusters is not always clearly defined; in some cases clustering is confused with more generic

---

Box 8.1

Interface between Government Policies to Support Micro, Small, and Medium Enterprises and Strategies to Develop Clusters in Cameroon

The severe economic crisis that occurred in the second half of the 1980s and the eventual adoption of the Structural Adjustment Program led the government to abandon the previous import substitution strategy. The economic crisis and the failure of many firms provided a breeding ground for small and medium enterprises (SMEs). Today, SMEs occupy an important place in the Cameroonian economy, making a significant contribution to GDP, employment, and poverty reduction. However, the economic liberalization that followed the adoption of the Structural Adjustment Program took away any form of government support to SMEs that had existed before. The financial institution created by government to provide and guarantee loans to such firms collapsed because of poor management. After several years of inaction, the government has initiated several strategies to develop the sector. The Ministry of Small and Medium-Sized Enterprises was created in 2004 and charged with designing and implementing policies aimed at developing SMEs. Prior to this, the Ministry of Industry and Trade had been in charge of SMEs. The creation of a separate ministry indicates the importance of the expanding SME sector in Cameroon's economy.

(continued next page)

Box 8.1 *(continued)*

The Priority Program for the Promotion of SMEs was created, with the assistance of the United Nations Development Programme, to map out a strategy for promoting SMEs in Cameroon. The government is also planning to add an agency for the development of SMEs and a development bank specifically to serve the financing needs of SMEs.

Many SMEs in Cameroon are found in the informal sector, where some take refuge for tax reasons. The government has no specific policies for informal sector activities. Firms in this sector might benefit from initiatives to build their capacity. All of the firms surveyed for this study are in the informal sector, and their clustering has not attracted policy interventions from the government. Enterprise clustering has been spontaneous. The Competitiveness Committee has a project to set up a cluster of SMEs, but the initiative will certainly exclude the informal firms surveyed for this study. The project will involve more formal firms with a reasonable level of capital able to produce and export to other countries. The intention of the Competitiveness Committee is to create a "new" cluster and not to build from existing informal sector clusters.

Source: Khan 2009.

Box 8.2

Interface between Government Policies to Support Micro, Small, and Medium Enterprises and Strategies to Develop Clusters in Kenya

Kenya's development strategy over the last two decades has focused on economic reforms, with the aim of achieving newly industrialized country status by 2020. The strategy focuses on market and trade liberalization, privatization of public corporations, export promotion, an outward-oriented economic strategy, reform of the interest rate regime, and reduction of deficit financing. To promote the development of micro and small enterprises (MSEs), Sessional Paper no. 2 of 2005 on MSEs was formulated. The main objectives are to identify the challenges that affect the development of the MSE sector, to lay down policies to address those challenges, to define the implementation plans, and to advise the government to allocate 25 percent of its procurement of goods and services to the MSE sector. The Kenyan government has also formulated other policy documents aimed at enhancing exports and investment. They include the National Export Strategy Paper, Trade and Industrial Policy, and Kenya's Industrial Master Plan (MAPSKID, the Master Plan Study for Kenya's Industrial Development). The National Export Strategy Paper seeks to increase Kenya's exports and competitiveness. The Trade and Industrial Policy aims to enhance and maintain Kenya's industrial competitiveness domestically, regionally, and internationally. MAPSKID seeks to promote industrial development in Kenya with an emphasis on targeted sectors, including agro-processing, agro-machinery, and electrics, electronics, and information and communications technology (ICT). The government is also formulating a Business Incubation Policy. By pursuing regional economic integration policy, Kenya also aims to exploit economies of scale, attract investments, improve resource allocation, and attract technology transfer.

The country's development strategy, as part of wider economic reforms, also focuses on attracting foreign direct investment (FDI) and portfolio investment. In this regard, economic reforms have been undertaken to ensure an enabling environment for trade and investment. To attract FDI, the government has offered a wide range of concessions and incentives, including tax holidays, easy repatriation of profits, deregulation of foreign exchange, expedition of business registration processes, the right to invest in any sector except defense, and foreign investors' entitlement to the same privileges afforded local investors. The Private Sector Development Strategy launched in January 2007 aims to create a conducive business environment for private sector growth by alleviating major constraints and facilitating private-public partnerships. It also aims to enhance the growth and competitiveness of the private sector, especially, micro, small, and medium enterprises.

Source: Akoten 2009.

Box 8.3

Interface between Government Policies to Support Micro, Small, and Medium Enterprises and Strategies to Develop Clusters in Ghana

The Ghanaian government in its proposed medium-term plan intends to use industrial clusters as part of the horizontal policy framework to develop the industrial sector. This policy strategy is founded on the basis that Ghanaian companies are fragmented and small and cannot use scale economies in competitive pricing. With the small-scale level of their operations, these SMEs are not able to access the resources needed to mass produce and be competitive. The creation of business and industrial clusters is intended to redress this situation. The proposed cluster initiatives would enable manufacturing enterprises to work together on a range of issues for the common good, improving their sustainability, competitiveness, and profitability. Areas of cooperation include the following:

- *Infrastructure.* SMEs located in the business cluster receive access roads, energy, water resources, and shared meeting or video-conferencing facilities to reduce transportation costs and negative environmental impacts.
- *Waste.* Businesses use waste as a resource to create new opportunities for other businesses. They also save costs by collaborating on the disposal and recycling of waste.
- *Networking.* Networking between SMEs pushes thinking on sustainable development, competitive practices, and cost reduction. Networking helps to formalize the exchange of ideas on sustainable development—for example, long-term thinking in support of new laws and regulations. A collective voice also means that SMEs can have a greater influence on sustainable development issues because they speak with one voice to influence government policy.
- *Inputs and suppliers.* SMEs collectively create demand by sourcing inputs locally and selling locally. SMEs cooperate on sustainable procurement by questioning where raw materials come from, buying in bulk to share among common enterprises, sharing the costs of training suppliers, and jointly raising standards.
- *Physical environment.* SMEs collaborate to improve their physical environment by improving the attractiveness of facilities, buildings, and cultural facilities. This involves not just SMEs within clusters but also the local communities in which they are located.

- *Employment.* SMEs work together to promote local employment, train local people, develop community groups, and promote research and development on sustainable development in universities.
- *Transport.* Businesses cooperate by pooling car parking, lift-sharing schemes, sharing rail or road freight, or collectively negotiating better public transport systems for the benefit of their employees and local community.

Source: Aryeetey, Owusu, and Quartey 2009.

Box 8.4

Interface between Government Policies to Support Micro, Small, and Medium Enterprises and Strategies to Develop Clusters in Rwanda

Small businesses are one of the most important impetuses for Rwanda's private sector development. SMEs account for 60 percent of GDP, 97 percent of firms, and 70 percent of employment in Rwanda. Most of these private enterprises are in the commerce and service sectors. Industrial activities are mainly import substitution, oriented toward the local market for basic products.

In order for small and medium enterprises and industry to grow, one of the key policy strategies is to promote linkages among enterprises as well as between enterprises and their institutional environment. Research evidence from developing and developed countries shows that competitive relations and joint action are necessary when enterprises operate in proximity. Close proximity enables firms to share business interests such as markets for products, infrastructure, and human capacity. Within such groups, or clusters, joint initiatives are stronger because there is a critical mass of interested parties, more cost-effective because they share fixed costs, and easier to coordinate because proximity fosters mutual knowledge and trust. The government of Rwanda, therefore, has launched an important strategy with the aim of developing capabilities at both the local and the national levels to promote networking and cluster development among small and medium enterprises and industry. In this regard, the Private Sector Federation is urging private sector members and stakeholders to consider how they can help one another strategically and technically to improve their businesses and strengthen the spirit of competitiveness by working in a cluster system.

(continued next page)

Box 8.4 *(continued)*

The government of Rwanda has long recognized that the ICT, coffee, tourism, and manufacturing sectors enable economic development. This is reflected in the government's Vision 2020, a plan that aims to transform Rwanda into an information-rich, knowledge-based society and economy by 2020. The infrastructural constraints on growth of the industrial sector in Rwanda are significant. Identification of the sectors and locations for infrastructural support is crucial if the limited resources are to be used efficiently and productively to raise the competitiveness of domestic enterprises. Against this background, Rwanda is launching cluster initiatives organizing coffee, tea, and tourism firms as well as new types of clusters like ICT, dairy, and mining. The number of clusters has grown, but most of them have not yet been studied.

Source: Musana and Murenzi 2009.

sector development strategies, with little clarity as to how players at various stages of the value chain will be linked. In particular, spontaneously formed industrial clusters are not in the picture.

Several countries in Africa are developing value chain strategies in the context of domestic private sector development. A cluster strategy and a value chain strategy are quite similar. The difference is that, while a value chain approach is transaction oriented and focuses on transactional efficiency within the chain, a cluster approach is more systemic. A cluster strategy includes analysis of a cluster's value chain and focuses on solving coordination and information failures through better participation of supporting institutions outside the value chain (World Bank 2009a). Cluster projects tend to involve the entire value chain plus any entity that has the potential to influence the cluster and beyond. Such entities include traders, processors, manufacturers, exporters, training institutes, and government standards bureaus.

Competitive value chains need to achieve not only efficiency along the value chain but also thickness of each layer, which is the basis for efficiency gains and sustainability. The agglomeration dynamics embedded in natural industrial clusters have the potential to contribute to such thickening of the layers. A cluster policy has to be based on market potential and designed to provide institutional support to clusters that makes sense economically. Natural clusters have grown spontaneously without public policy support. The vast majority of clusters in Africa are surviving at the subsistence level. What they lack is competitiveness, depth, innovation, and the capability to upgrade.

The role of public policies in developing clusters also needs to be approached carefully so as not to undermine natural economic forces of agglomeration and endogenous innovation and knowledge spillover. Policy interventions intended to create physical hardware alone, without building a sound incentive framework for the private sector, have often failed, as have many export-processing zones in Africa as well as some cluster development initiatives. In some cases, like Zhangjiang Hi-Tech Park in Shanghai, China, agglomeration occurred due to subsidized land and buildings, but in different industries from those originally planned.[1]

In the process of cluster development, government and the private sector interplay with each other. The nature of the interplay varies among different examples of cluster development around the world (see boxes 8.5 and 8.6 for examples of regional experiences in South and East Asia and Latin America, respectively). In some cases, governments have taken more active roles at early stages of cluster development

---

Box 8.5

Role of Public Policies in Industrial Clusters in South and East Asia

Industrial clusters have evolved naturally in South and East Asia, which can be attributed somewhat to these regions being among the most highly populated areas in the world. Only a few of these naturally formed clusters, however, have been able to make the transition into advanced clusters that contribute significantly to the home economy and are fully integrated with the global standards of exports and technology.

Several natural industrial clusters are in South Asia. For example, the vast Indian subcontinent has given rise to regionally specialized clusters for the performing arts as well as clusters for the production of art objects, with distinct regional compositions. Some of India's specialized textile and leather industries are clustered in cities like Agra, Banaras, and Rajasthan. However, these have few lessons

(continued next page)

Box 8.5 *(continued)*

for public policy because they were often organized in introverted ways and make little contribution to integrating the local and global economies. Banerjee and Nihila (1999) have compared the leather clusters in Agra and Chennai to discuss the degree of introversion and extroversion in Indian industrial clusters. They conclude that, even when clusters are extroverted, as in the case of the Chennai leather cluster, they rely little on public policy inputs. Similar conclusions can be drawn from the formidable Indian ICT cluster in South India, which is attributed more to the technological skills and astuteness of IT entrepreneurs than to the effectiveness of public policies, at least in the cluster's formative stage.

The Bangladeshi ready-made garment cluster also grew despite government indifference, although it benefited from the Multi-Fibre Arrangement, which gave Bangladeshi garments privileged access to the U.S. market. Although the two special economic zones in Dhaka and Chittagong are important industrial clusters, several other industrial clusters around Dhaka are not confined to common premises as special economic zones but still undertake important joint actions and make important contributions to the global and local economies. Some of these clusters—for example, the one in Narayangunj—have benefited greatly from joint actions undertaken to sensitize public policies to their industrial needs. But the role of the private sector is still more important than that of the public sector in the formation and maintenance of clusters.

The South Asian experience contrasts with that of East Asia. Governments in East Asia including China have a high-profile role in the initial stages of cluster planning, such as guiding the cluster mapping, and in the final stages, such as leading public-private dialogue on policy and institutional bottlenecks that inhibit industry development and the business environment. The governments often assume a lower profile during intermediate stages, such as the analysis of firm-level competitiveness and market and product segmentation. But the role of governments is paramount in the development of public goods that form the basis for industrial clusters, such as technology enhancement, skill development, and infrastructure development.

Source: Mallika Shakya contributed this box.

and have led the private sector in developing clusters. In other cases, governments have provided support to existing clusters that were formed as a result of private sector initiatives. There is no one-size-fits-all formula as to how governments and the private sector should interplay and those examples should be interpreted in specific country and sectoral contexts.

Box 8.6

Role of Public Policies in Industrial Clusters in Latin America

In many of the Latin American countries where clusters have successfully developed and reached worldwide presence, the role of the public sector has been significant. In Brazil, for example, in one of the most dynamic and productive fruit
clusters, the government has been a catalyst in helping to create the infrastructure necessary for the cluster to develop as well as in providing loans through the
national development bank for the promotion of firms in the region. Costa Rica,
which showcases one of the most dynamic clusters in electronics and IT in the
region, benefited from a great push by President José María Figueres, whose
government committed to a sustainable development strategy in which cluster
development played a major role. The strategy eventually brought Intel to the
country, helping to foster the electronics and IT cluster.

However, there is also some heterogeneity in the development of clusters in
the region. For example, the salmon cluster in Chile developed with less pronounced government influence, and the maquila sector in Chihuahua, Mexico,
developed mainly through the commitment of the private sector. The cluster in
Chihuahua eventually evolved into a public-private partnership. However, cluster
development in the region has generally begun with a public sector initiative,
sometimes in a more subsidiary way and in other cases in a more leading manner.

Most clusters in Latin America, with a few exceptions found in middle-income
countries, also differ to various degrees from the complex and innovative clusters
of developed countries, as many authors have highlighted. In most clusters in the
industrial world, SMEs play an important role as providers of specialized inputs
and services. In contrast, in Latin American clusters, the vast majority of SMEs are
not competitive. Modern large firms may coexist with SMEs, but the cooperation
between parties is much less pronounced, due in large part to a technological
gap. Training is not advanced, and firms at the same level cooperate in a restrict-
ed manner, often because cultural issues limit their ability to cooperate. With
significant exceptions in middle-income countries, the region still struggles to
create locally owned, innovative industries based on scientific and technological knowledge.

Lately, within the region, nongovernmental stakeholders involved in clusters,
competitiveness, and innovation programs are increasingly pushing the agenda
and contributing to an open dialogue and dissemination of best practices within
the region. One clear initiative on this path is the Latin American Cluster Network

(continued next page)

Box 8.6 *(continued)*

(RedLAC), which maintains a regional dialogue on competitiveness, clusters, and innovation for economic development in Latin America through the exchange of experiences and best practices. RedLAC is part of TCI, the global practitioners' network for competitiveness, clusters, and innovation. What makes clusters so attractive for policy makers and practitioners in Latin American countries are the opportunities for collective efficiency and improved competitiveness that emanate from a combination of positive external economies, low transaction costs, and joint action.

Source: Manuella Frota contributed this box.

Public policies do play an important role in cluster development by providing essential public goods. What is important is to carefully balance cluster-targeted policies with spatially blind, sectorally blind improvements in investment climates and provisions of public goods so as not to introduce excessive distortions to the economy. Such policies need to be designed to enhance the private sector incentives in investing and trading rather than go against them. Public-private dialogue is crucial in designing cluster strategies in this context.

The following spatially blind, sectorally blind policies are particularly closely linked to the development of industrial clusters.

Managerial Skill Development. While more targeted managerial skill development programs for industrial clusters have merit, such interventions must be complemented by a national effort to strengthen formal education, particularly secondary and vocational education. In building a stronger domestic private sector, education is critically important to developing a solid base of entrepreneurship in the country. Efforts should be made not only by the government but also by the private sector to build better linkages between higher education and private businesses that would help to make business a viable career option based on a better understanding of how the private and public sector labor markets interplay.

Infrastructure to Improve Connectivity and Facilitate Cross-Border Trade. Improved connectivity by means of transport and communication infrastructure at the national level would significantly reduce the transaction costs of doing business. Infrastructure support to specific clusters should be complemented by national efforts to close the infrastructure gap and ensure that cluster-based enterprises are well connected with external markets within the country or with other countries through exports and imports. The facilitation of cross-border trade with neighboring countries through improvements in customs, transport, and market information infrastructure, particularly at the regional level, also helps to strengthen the market access of micro and small enterprises.

Policies to Encourage the Formation of Business Associations. In developing new market opportunities, business associations play a pivotal role in facilitating the ability of cluster-based enterprises to form horizontal networks and take "joint actions" to develop new markets and find collaborative solutions to market access constraints, such as joint investments in facilities to provide the certification of product quality required by overseas markets. Associations also help to formulate public-private partnerships and to facilitate public support such as security, land, and infrastructure, particularly in the areas of power and transport. Business associations also provide BDS.

Policies to Improve Access to Credit among Micro and Small Enterprises. Improving access to credit is another critically important area for micro and small enterprises seeking to reach out to new markets. Strengthening microfinance institutions is clearly a high priority for many governments. African governments can increase access to microfinance by encouraging competition in order to drive intermediaries to reach and serve more clients. Governments must also take care not to overregulate the microfinance industry. Some microfinance institutions in developing countries offer BDS to their clients in order to improve the viability and growth of SMEs. Studies show that linking microfinance institutions and BDS providers would improve the chances of success for SMEs in developing countries. When microfinance is tied to BDS, the firm owners who use both services perform substantially better than those who receive only microfinance.

Note

1. Shanghai Zhangjiang Hi-Tech Park, founded in July 1992, was originally intended to create a biomedical cluster linked to Shanghai University of Traditional Chinese Medicine. However, an insufficient number of enterprises in the biomedical industry showed interest in becoming tenants in the park. In August 1999 the Shanghai Municipal Committee and Municipal Government introduced the strategy, Focus on Zhangjiang, and identified information and communications technology, software, and biomedicine as the leading industries to be located in the park. These industries would play a leading role in innovation, allowing other industries to become tenants.

Since then, Zhangjiang has developed rapidly. Currently, the park houses seven industries, six of which are related to electronics and information technology (including integrated circuits), biomedicine, software, creative industry, bank cards, photoelectrons, and the China Eastern Information Security Industry Park.

References

Akoten, John. 2009. "Industrial Clusters and Indigenous Private Sector in Africa: The Case of Kenya." Background technical paper prepared for the study.

Akoten, John, and Keijiro Otsuka. 2007. "From Tailors to Mini-Manufacturers: The Role of Traders in the Transformation of Garment Enterprises in Kenya." *Journal of African Economies* 16 (4): 564–95.

Aryeetey, Ernest, George Owusu, and Peter Quartey. 2009. "Industrial Clusters and Indigenous Private Sector in Africa: Ghana Case Study." Background technical paper prepared for the study.

Banerjee, Nirmala, and Millie Nihila. 1999. "Business Organisation in Leather Industries of Calcutta and Chennai." In *Economy and Organisation: Indian Industries under the Neo-liberal Regime*, ed. Amiya K. Bagchi. New Delhi: Sage Publications.

Khan, Sunday. 2009. "Industrial Clusters and Indigenous Private Sector in Africa: Cameroon Country Case Study." Background technical paper prepared for the study.

Musana, Serge, and Ivan Murenzi. 2009. "Industrial Clusters and Indigenous Private Sector in Africa: The Case of Rwanda." Background technical paper prepared for the study.

Oyelaran-Oyeyinka, Banji, and Dorothy McCormick, eds. 2007. *Industrial Clusters and Innovation Systems in Africa*. Tokyo: United Nations University Press.

Sonobe, Tetsushi, and Keijiro Otsuka. 2006. *Cluster-Based Industrial Development: An East Asian Model*. New York: Palgrave Macmillan.

World Bank. 2009a. *Cluster Initiatives for Competitiveness: A Practical Guide and Toolkit*. Washington, DC: World Bank.

———. 2009b. *World Development Report 2009: Reshaping Economic Geography*. Washington, DC: World Bank.

Yoshino, Yutaka. 2008. "Domestic Constraints, Firm Characteristics, and Geographical Diversification of Firm-Level Manufacturing Exports in Africa." Policy Research Working Paper 4574, World Bank, Washington, DC.

Instrumental Variable Model Estimation on Domestic Ownership Effect on Productivity

Dependent variable: value added per worker (log)

Independent variable	(I)	(II)	(III)	(IV)	(V)
Domestic ownership	−0.609***	−0.551***	−0.375***	−0.350***	−0.228***
	(0.056)	(0.057)	(0.084)	(0.074)	(0.074)
Manager's postsecondary education		0.345***	0.091	0.056	0.075
		(0.044)	(0.072)	(0.063)	(0.056)
Access to formal finance			2.657***	2.113***	1.284**
			(0.434)	(0.422)	(0.587)
Capital intensity				0.157***	0.162***
				(0.019)	(0.018)
Nonlocal market sales					0.809***
					(0.308)
Number of observations	3,767	3,764	3,318	3,318	3,159
R^2	0.364	0.374	−0.158 C	0.104 C	0.287 C
			0.914 U	0.933 U	0.948 U

	(VI)	(VII)	(VIII)	(IX)	(X)
Domestic ownership	−0.421***	−0.396***	−0.386***	−0.342***	−0.163*
	(0.059)	(0.060)	(0.065)	(0.061)	(0.093)
Size (small)	−0.265***	−0.222***	−0.089	−0.095	0.271*
	(0.042)	(0.043)	(0.086)	(0.076)	(0.154)
Size (large)	0.265***	0.250***	0.152*	0.155**	−0.393**
	(0.064)	(0.064)	(0.085)	(0.076)	(0.199)

	(VI)	(VII)	(VIII)	(IX)	(X)
Manager's postsecondary education		0.254*** (0.045)	0.213*** (0.056)	0.141*** (0.050)	0.063 (0.070)
Access to formal finance			1.00* (0.527)	0.611 (0.484)	1.033 (0.669)
Capital intensity				0.197*** (0.017)	0.146*** (0.027)
Nonlocal market sales					2.102*** (0.694)
Number of observations	3,564	3,562	3,318	3,318	3,159
R^2	0.384	0.390	0.337 C 0.951 U	0.449 C 0.959 U	−0.036 C 0.924 U

Source: Feng, Mengistae, and Yoshino 2009.
Note: Country and sector dummies are included, but not reported. C = centered R^2. U = uncentered R^2.
*** $p < 0.01$.
** $p < 0.05$.
* $p < 0.10$.

Reference

Feng, Juan, Taye Mengistae, and Yutaka Yoshino. 2009. "Foreign Premium on Productivity among Enterprises in Africa." Analytical background note prepared for the study.

Basic Characteristics of Sampled Micro and Small Light Manufacturing Enterprises Inside and Outside the Clusters

Characteristic	All three industries		Metal and machinery		Textiles and garments		Wood and furniture	
	Inside	Outside	Inside	Outside	Inside	Outside	Inside	Outside
Number of observations	198	158	43	35	64	73	91	50
Median sales per worker ($ purchasing power parity)	4,124.5	2,566.7	2,760.0	2,464.0	2,392.1	2,337.3	6,400.0	3,140.0
Median capital per worker ($ purchasing power parity)	1,065.5	799.1	2,566.7	1,100.0	998.9	998.9	837.0	567.7
% of enterprises with managers with postsecondary education	41.4	52.5	69.8	71.4	39.1	45.2	29.7	50.0
% of enterprises with managers with a university degree	2.5	9.5	0.0	0.0	6.3	20.5	1.1	0.0
Mean age of enterprises	12.1	10.2	11.5	12.5	11.8	10.4	12.7	8.4
% of enterprises with a female owner	15.7	22.2	2.3	2.9	35.9	32.9	7.7	20.0
% of enterprises with a foreign owner	2.5	1.9	0.0	2.9	7.8	1.4	0.0	2.0

% of enterprises with access to formal finance	19.7	14.6	7.0	11.4	21.9	15.1	24.2	16.0
% of enterprises purchasing inputs outside of local markets	13.6	5.7	7.0	14.3	10.9	4.1	18.7	2.0
% of enterprises selling products outside of local markets	75.3	41.1	88.4	60.0	82.8	35.6	63.7	36.0
% of enterprises exporting their products	22.2	8.9	30.2	5.7	14.1	11.0	24.2	8.0
Mean % of sales sold outside of local markets	26.7	8.8	34.1	12.4	26.5	6.4	23.4	9.9
Mean % of sales exported	3.0	0.5	2.6	1.4	2.2	0.1	3.7	0.4
Mean number of total workers	4.4	3.5	5.5	4.1	3.8	3.1	4.4	3.6
Mean ratio of apprentices to permanent workers	1.4	1.8	2.4	1.8	0.9	1.9	1.3	1.8

Source: Authors.

APPENDIX 3

Data Envelopment Analysis

Two variables are used to capture the performance of enterprises. This study uses a nonparametric frontier model—data envelopment analysis (DEA)—to measure the cost efficiency of an individual enterprise. The cost efficiency is further decomposed into two components: technical efficiency and allocative efficiency. On the basis of an input-saving efficiency measure, DEA is expressed as follows:

$$Min\, \theta_s \; st \; \sum_{s=1}^{S} \lambda_s y_{is} > y_{is} \quad i = 1,...,m, \;\; s = 1,...,S, \qquad \text{(C.1)}$$

$$\sum_{s=1}^{S} \lambda_s x_{is} \leq \theta_s x_{is} \quad j = 1,...,n,$$

$$\lambda_i \geq 0, \sum_{s=1}^{S} \lambda_s = 1$$

where θ = efficiency score, representing the fraction by which an observation can multiply its input vector and still produce no less of any output, y = output vectors, x = input vectors, and λ = intensity vector forming convex combinations of output vectors and input vectors.

Figure A3.1   Data Envelopment Analysis and the Distance Function

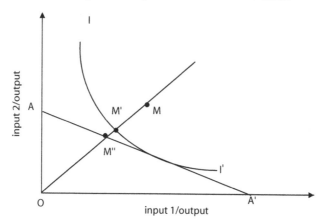

Source: Authors.

The basic concept is illustrated on the basis of the distance function, as shown in figure A3.1. The units M' lying on the isoquant represented by $I\,I'$ are the fully efficient enterprises, indicating that the firm uses fewer inputs to produce the same amount of output. If a given enterprise uses quantities of inputs, defined by point M, to produce a unit of output, the technical inefficiency of the firm is presented by the distance MM', which suggests that the inputs could be reduced without the reduction in output. The technical efficiency (TE) of an enterprise is measured by the ratio of the distance OM' to distance OM. Therefore, the total efficiency is expressed as follows:

$$TE_i = OM' / OM \tag{C.2}$$

Therefore, TE takes a value between 0 and 1, with 1 indicating that the enterprise is technically efficient. In addition to TE, Farrell (1957) introduces allocative efficiency (AE), measured as the ratio of the distance OM'' to distance OM':

$$AE_i = OM'' / OM' \tag{C.3}$$

Total efficiency (EE) is calculated by multiplying technical efficiency by allocative efficiency. Hence EE is measured as follows:

$$EE_s = TE_s \times AE_s = OM'' / OM \tag{C.4}$$

Reference

Farrell, M. J. 1957. "The Measurement of Productive Efficiency." *Journal of the Royal Statistical Society* 120 (3): 253–81.

Format of Managerial Skills Training Programs

In each cluster in the study, the managerial training program comprised three weeks of classroom instruction in two- to three-hour sessions per day from Monday to Friday. The program was offered strictly to owners and managers of enterprises in the cluster. No workers or apprentices were allowed to participate. The sessions were organized after normal business hours (late afternoon to evening hours) to accommodate managers' work schedules.

Each program consisted of three modules: (1) entrepreneurship, business strategy, and marketing (module 1); (2) production management and quality assurance (module 2); and (3) record keeping and business financial documents (module 3). See box A4.1 for the list of topics covered in each module. The technical level was very elementary and tailored to participants without prior knowledge of modern management techniques. A more critical prerequisite for this training program was experience in enterprise management.

The same format and training materials were applied in both clusters with slight local customization of the contents (for example, types of examples used in the interactive sessions).[1] The training sessions were conducted in English based on the training materials, including PowerPoint presentations in English. Interpreters were hired for the training to

Box A4.1

Outline of the Managerial Training Programs

Module 1. Entrepreneurship, business strategy, and marketing

Day 1. Introduction: expression of expectations, course overview, entrepreneurial competencies

Day 2. Entrepreneurial competencies and cluster groups: concept of collaboration in a cluster group, business's role in the supply chain and adding value

Day 3. Competitiveness: how to build a competitive business, what it takes to build a competitive business

Day 4. Marketing: identify buyer priorities (serve the demand), segment the market, position the offer

Day 5. Business strategy: putting a strategy together, drafting a strategy element for a business plan

Module 2. Production management and quality assurance

Day 1. Overview of production management and quality assurance: overview of the module, establishing what is production and management, introduction to production management and quality management, establishing the purpose and need, drafting an element of the business plan (business focus)

Day 2. Production planning: how to organize the production process; planning for requirements in production, labor, materials, and equipment; allocating time and time management

Day 3. Quality assurance: designing techniques and steps to follow in production, equipment, labor, and what it takes to assure quality, contribution of the cluster to quality (standards and peer regulation)

Day 4. Productivity improvement: problem solving, team building, removing factors that lower productivity, reducing waste

Day 5. The five Ss of quality management: sort, systemize, sweep, standardize, self-discipline

Module 3. Record keeping and business financial documents

Day 1. Importance and uses of record keeping: overview of the module, importance and types of record keeping and financial documentation, linking this module to the earlier modules

Day 2. Types of record keeping: identification of different types of costs, identification of different types of records to keep, how to keep proper records

Day 3. Costing and pricing of products and services: identifying and calculating different types of costs pricing, developing cluster purchasing power (power to reduce input costs), determining break-even price or quantity, drafting financials (elements of a business plan)

Day 4. Cash flow management: how to manage cash, how to develop a cash flow budget (element of a business plan), how to manage working capital

Day 5. Meeting legal requirements and understanding financial statements: income statement (element of a business plan), balance sheet (element of a business plan), legal requirement of paying tax and value added tax

Sources: EDC Limited 2008, 2007.

respond to occasional requests from participants for translation services between English and the local language (that is, Kiswahili in Kariobangi Light Industries and Twi in Suame Magazine).

The training program was also very participatory and interactive. Each day's presentation was preceded by feedback from participants on areas needing improvement and corrections with respect to general organization. This was followed by a recap of the previous day's lesson aimed at establishing participants' understanding of the subjects taught. The day's lessons were then presented in a participatory session of exercises, discussions, reviews, and questions. This approach allowed all participants to share their experiences and opinions.[2]

Overall, the results of these assessments indicate that participants understood what was being taught. For example, the average test score was 71 percent in Kariobangi and 65 percent in Suame Magazine. However, understanding the importance and the workings of record keeping and other business techniques is not enough to improve business performance. These business activities are effective only if entrepreneurs make them a part of their daily business routine.

In each cluster, slightly fewer than 50 participants completed the entire three-week program. The attendance rate was high (93 percent on average in Kariobangi and 89 percent on average in Suame Magazine).

In Suame Magazine, randomization was relatively easy. All of the entrepreneurs, except car mechanics and blacksmiths who were covered by the baseline survey as presented in Iddrisu, Mano, and Sonobe (2009), were informed by means of a flyer of the upcoming training program before and during the summer of 2007. Out of 200 entrepreneurs in the initial list (limited to machinists and manufacturers), 57 were admitted to the training based on random selection, of which 48 attended the program until the end. Randomization could not be done properly in Kariobangi. Similar to Suame Magazine, the target group of entrepreneurs was informed of the training program during the summer of 2007. However, violence erupted after the presidential election in late December 2007, and implementation of the training program had to be delayed from January to April 2008; this delay reduced awareness and motivation among the target group of entrepreneurs for the program. The selection of participants, including a re-sensitization effort, was further disrupted by a series of local security incidents in Nairobi, including some in Kariobangi itself, that occurred immediately before the start date of the training program.[3] Only 60 entrepreneurs applied to the program in Kariobangi (among 127 entrepreneurs participating in the baseline survey who were informed of the program), and all were admitted to the program. Thus participation was purely by self-selection.

Notes

1. The only exception is that a guest speaker from a bank was invited to speak to participants in Kenya, while no guest speaker was invited in Ghana. The speaker was from the Equity Bank of Kenya and made a presentation on the bank's products and services and its credit appraisal process.

2. In-class teaching was complemented by on-site coaching provided upon request. In each country, 15 entrepreneurs were selected to receive on-site assessment and coaching. During the module training, the instructor or resource person would visit enterprises to discuss specific problems and to coach managers to develop solutions.

3. The start of the training program itself was also delayed by two days.

References

EDC Limited. 2007. "Training Report: Implementation of Pilot Cluster Business Management Training Programs in Ghana (Kumasi)." Consultancy report, World Bank, Washington, DC.

———. 2008. "Training Report: Implementation of Pilot Cluster Business Management Training Programs in Kenya (Nairobi)." Consultancy report, World Bank, Washington, DC.

Iddrisu, Alhassan, Yukichi Mano, and Tetsushi Sonobe. 2009. "Entrepreneurial Skills and Industrial Development: The Case of a Car Repair and Metalworking Cluster in Ghana." Centre for the Study of African Economies, Department of Economics, Oxford University (February 27).

Average Treatment of Treated and DID Matching Estimator

Let D_i be a dummy variable indicating whether entrepreneur i participates in the training program. The changes in business routines and performance of entrepreneur i are denoted by $\Delta Y_i(D_i) = Y_{ia}(D_i) - Y_{ib}(D_i)$, where subscripts a and b denote "after" and "before" the entrepreneur training, respectively. The outcome variable $\Delta Y_i(D_i)$ depends on whether or not the entrepreneur participates in the training. The individual effect of the entrepreneur training on the changes in business routines and performance is given by $\Delta Y_i(1) - \Delta Y_i(0)$.

The major difficulty in examining this effect is that $\Delta Y_i(0)$ is not observable if entrepreneur i participates in the training, and $\Delta Y_i(1)$ is not observable if entrepreneur i does not participate in the training. Thus we focus on estimating the average effect of treatment on the treated (ATT), defined as

$$ATT = E\left[\Delta Y_i(1)|D_i = 1, X_i\right] - E\left[\Delta Y_i(0)|D_i = 1, X_i\right] \tag{E.1}$$

where X_i denotes the observed characteristics of entrepreneur i before the training. The first term on the right-hand side of the equation can be estimated by the average change in an outcome of the training participants, whereas the second term represents the counterfactual change in an outcome that training participant i would have achieved if the entrepreneur had not participated in the training. If participation in the training had been randomized, it would have been possible to estimate this counterfactual by averaging changes in the outcomes of nonparticipants. Since participation in the training was not randomized, we are concerned with the estimation bias due to self-selection into participation. The self-selection may be correlated with the observed characteristics of the entrepreneurs, even though it may also be correlated with unobserved characteristics. However, using the data envelopement analysis (DID) matching estimator, ATT is equal to

$$ATT = E\ [\Delta Y_i(1)|D_i = 1,\ X_i] - E\ [\Delta Y_i(0)|D_i = 0,\ X_i] \qquad \text{(E.2)}$$

Two different DID matching methods were employed to check the robustness of the estimation results: one is the DID propensity score matching (PSM) estimator based on local linear matching proposed by Heckman, Ichimura, and Todd (1997, 1998), and the other is a DID version of the bias-corrected matching (BCM) estimator based on nearest-neighbor matching with replacement proposed by Abadie and others (2004) and Abadie and Imbens (2006, 2007). These matching methods have been widely applied to nonexperimental data from developing economies (Diaz and Handa 2006; Mano and others 2009). For example, Rosholm, Nielsen, and Dabalen (2007) use the PSM to evaluate the impacts on labor productivity of technical training programs for workers in Kenya and Zambia, and Behrman, Parker, and Todd (2009) use both DID-PSM and DID-BCM to evaluate the impacts on schooling of conditional cash transfers for young children in Mexico.

The DID-PSM estimator can be generally expressed as

$$DID\text{-}PSM = \frac{1}{N_1} \sum_{i \in I_1} \left[\Delta Y_i(1) - \sum_{j \in I_0} W\big(p(X_i),\ p(X_j)\big) \Delta Y_j(0) \right] \qquad \text{(E.3)}$$

where I_1 and I_0 are, respectively, the participant and the matched nonparticipant group, N_1 is the number of participants, $p(X_i)$ is the propensity score or the probability of training participation conditional on characteristics X_i, and the function W gives a greater weight to nonparticipant j with the propensity score closer to participant i's propensity score and a lower weight to a nonparticipant at a distance. Analogously, the DID-BCM can be expressed as follows:

$$DID \text{-} BCM = \frac{1}{N_1} \sum_{i \in I_1} \left[\Delta Y_i(1) \Delta \tilde{Y}_i(0) \right] \qquad \text{(E.4)}$$

where $\Delta \tilde{Y}_i(0) = \Delta Y_j(0) + \hat{\mu}_0(X_i) - \hat{\mu}_0(X_j)$, j denotes the closest match on covariates X for unit i. The function $\hat{\mu}_0$ is a fitted linear regression function of ΔY on covariates X. It is used to adjust the counterfactual estimates to account for differences in X between each participant and the matched nonparticipant, which otherwise lead to biased estimates (Abadie and Imbens 2006, 2007).

Following Heckman, Ichimura, and Todd (1997), we reduce potential bias as much as possible by matching training participants with nonparticipants operating the same type of manufacturing business in the same geographic area and using the data for both participants and nonparticipants in the same survey, in which the same questionnaire was used for participants and nonparticipants.

The covariates used for matching are time-invariant or come from the pretraining period, that is, years of operation, age, years of schooling, working experience in the formal sector, and participation in past formal trainings. In estimating the propensity score, we perform the balancing tests proposed by Dehejia and Wahba (1999, 2002) to guide the specification of the probit model. They suggest adding interaction and higher-order terms to our base model until tests for mean differences in covariates between training participants and matched nonparticipants become statistically insignificant. We add higher-order terms of entrepreneur's age and interaction terms for participation in other training. In order to judge whether matching is successful, we rely on the t-test of equality in the mean of each covariate between the participants and nonparticipants and the pseudo R^2 and likelihood ratios obtained from estimating the probit model of participation. If matching is successful, the after-matching probit should have no explanatory power, whereas the before-matching probit should have explanatory power as long as selection on observables exists.

References

Abadie, Alberto, David Drukker, Jane Herr, and Guido Imbens. 2004. "Implementing Matching Estimators for Average Treatment Effects in Stata." *Stata Journal* 4 (3): 290–311.

Abadie, Alberto, and Guido Imbens. 2006. "Large Sample Properties of Matching Estimators for Average Treatment Effects." *Econometrica* 74 (1): 235–67.

———. 2007. "Bias Corrected Matching Estimators for Average Treatment Effects." Unpublished mss., Harvard University, Cambridge, MA.

Behrman, Jere R., Susan W. Parker, and Petra E. Todd. 2009. "Schooling Impacts of Conditional Cash Transfers on Young Children: Evidence from Mexico." *Economic Development and Cultural Change* 57 (3): 439–78.

Dehejia, Rajeev, and Sadek Wahba. 1999. "Causal Effects in Non-Experimental Studies: Re-Evaluating the Evaluation of Training Programs." *Journal of the American Statistical Association* 94 (448): 1053–62.

———. 2002. "Propensity Score Matching Methods for Non-Experimental Causal Studies." *Review of Economics and Statistics* 84 (1): 151–61.

Diaz, Jose J., and Sudhanshu Handa. 2006. "An Assessment of Propensity Score Matching as a Nonexperimental Impact Estimator: Evidence from Mexico's PROGRESA Program." *Journal of Human Resources* 41 (2): 319–45.

Heckman, James J., Hidehiko Ichimura, and Petra Todd. 1997. "Matching as an Econometric Evaluation Estimator: Evidence from Evaluating a Job Training Programme." *Review of Economic Studies* 64 (4): 605–54.

———. 1998. "Matching as an Econometric Evaluation Estimator." *Review of Economic Studies* 65 (2): 261–94.

Mano, Yukichi, John Akoten, Keijiro Otsuka, and Tetsushi Sonobe. 2009. "Impacts of Managerial Training: The Case of a Metalworking Cluster in Nairobi." Background technical paper prepared for the study.

Rosholm, Michael, Helena Skyt Nielsen, and Andrew Dabalen. 2007. "Evaluation of Training in African Enterprises." *Journal of Development Economics* 84 (1): 310–29.

List of Background Papers and Boxes Contributed for the Study

Type of study and title	Authors	Related chapter
Analytical notes		
1 Foreign Premium on Productivity among Enterprises in Africa	Juan Feng, Taye Mengistae, Yutaka Yoshino	2
2 Drivers of Market Participation: Does Being Indigenous Matter?	Rosanna Chan	2
3 Industrial Clusters in Developing Countries: A Conceptual Framework from Spatial Economics Perspective	Yutaka Yoshino	3
4 Industrial Clusters and Micro- and Small Light Manufacturing Enterprises in Africa: Findings from Country Case Studies	Theophile Bougna, Yutaka Yoshino	4, 5, 6
5 Location Choice and the Performance of Furniture Workshops in Arusha, Tanzania	Megumi Muto, Yessica C. Y. Chung, Shinobu Shimokoshi	5
6 Managerial Skills and Micro- and Small-Scale Enterprises in Industrial Clusters in Africa: Insights from Experimental Managerial Training in Ghana and Kenya	John Akoten, Yukichi Mano, Keijiro Otsuka, Tetsushi Sonobe, Yutaka Yoshino	7
Technical consultancy reports		
1 Training Report: Implementation of Pilot Cluster Business Management Training Programs in Ghana (Kumasi)	EDC Limited	7
2 Training Report: Implementation of Pilot Cluster Business Management Training Programs in Kenya (Nairobi)	EDC Limited	7
3 An Impact Evaluation of Managerial Training in Sub-Saharan Africa: A Case Study of a Metalworking Cluster in Kumasi	Yukichi Mano, Alhassan Iddrisu, Yutaka Yoshino, Tetsushi Sonobe	7
4 Impacts of Managerial Training: The Case of a Metalworking Cluster in Nairobi	Yukichi Mano, John Akoten, Keijiro Otsuka, Tetsushi Sonobe	7
5 Industrial Clusters and Indigenous Private Sector in Africa: The Case of Kenya	John Akoten (for Institute of Policy Analysis and Research Kenya)	4, 7, 8
6 Industrial Clusters and Indigenous Private Sector in Africa: The Case of Rwanda	Serge Musana, Ivan Murenzi (for Institute of Policy Analysis and Research Rwanda)	4, 8
7 Industrial Clusters and Indigenous Private Sector in Africa: Cameroon Country Case Study	Sunday Khan	6, 8
8 Industrial Clusters and Indigenous Private Sector in Africa: Ghana Case Study	Ernest Aryeetey, George Owusu, Peter Quartey (for Institute of Statistical Social and Economic Research)	3, 4, 8
Other boxes		
1 IT and IT-Enabled Services Clusters in Africa and around the World	Michael Engman	4
2 Role of Public Policies in Industrial Clusters in South and East Asia	Mallika Shakya	8
3 Role of Public Policies in Industrial Clusters in Latin America	Manuella Frota	8

Source: Authors.

174

Index

Boxes, figures, notes, and tables are indicated by *b*, *f*, *n*, and *t*, respectively. For specific clusters, check under the country name—the Arusha furniture cluster will be found under Tanzania, for instance.

A

access to finance. *See* finance, access to

access to markets. *See* external markets, access to

Africa. *See* Sub-Saharan Africa, and specific countries

African Economic Research Consortium, xiv, 65, 91

African Growth and Opportunity Act, U.S., 39*n*10

agglomeration, economic geography of, 43, 47–49, 49*f*

agricultural clusters, 82–84

Akoten, John, 55, 58, 108, 143

Altenburg, Tilman, 44, 53

Angola

    aggregate sales and number of enterprises by size of firm, 24*n*4

    labor productivity by sales and value added per worker, 25

Arab Republic of Egypt, as services outsourcing hub, 86*b*

Artadi, Elasa, 42

Asia. *See* East Asia; South Asia; specific countries

average treatment of treated and DID matching estimator, 169–72

B

backward linkage effect, 48, 49*f*, 56, 61*n*4

Banerjee, Nirmala, 152*b*

Bangladesh, ready-made garment cluster in, 152*b*

BDS (business development services), 114, 134, 141, 144, 155

Biggs, Tyler, 61*n*5

Blinder-Oaxaca decomposition technique

    cluster versus non-cluster-based enterprises, 68, 71*t*

    domestic versus foreign firms, 32–34, 32*b*, 33–34*f*

Botswana

    aggregate sales and number of enterprises by size of firm, 24*n*4

    labor productivity by sales and value added per worker, 25

    World Bank Doing Business report, ranking in, 24*n*3

Brazil, Sinos shoe cluster, 58